turning homeward

turning homeward

restoring hope and nature in the urban wild

adrienne ross scanlan

MOUNTAINEERS
BOOKS

MOUNTAINEERS BOOKS

Mountaineers Books is the publishing division of
The Mountaineers, an organization founded in 1906
and dedicated to the exploration, preservation, and
enjoyment of outdoor and wilderness areas.

1001 SW Klickitat Way, Suite 201, Seattle, WA 98134
800.553.4453, www.mountaineersbooks.org

Printed in the United States of America
Distributed in the United Kingdom by Cordee, www.cordee.co.uk
20 19 18 17 16   1 2 3 4 5

Copy Editor: Elizabeth Johnson
Design and layout: Jane Jeszeck/www.jigsawseattle.com
Front cover illustration: Copyright © 2016 by Linda Feltner
Interior and back cover illustrations: Copyright © 2016 by Elara Tanguy

Many of the essays in this book originally appeared, in different form, in the following
publications: *Tiny Lights, EarthLight, American Nature Writing 1997, American Nature Writing 2000,*
the *Fourth River, Raven Chronicles, Many Mountains Moving, EarthSpeak Magazine, Sugar Mule's* special
issue "Women Writing Nature," *An Orange County Almanac and Other Essays, City Creatures Blog,
Platte Valley Review*, and *The Prentice Hall Reader*, 11th edition.

Excerpt from "Some Thoughts on the Common Toad" from *The Orwell Reader*.
Copyright © 1949 by Houghton Mifflin Harcourt Publishing Company;
copyright © renewed 1977 by Sonia Orwell, reprinted by permission of Houghton
Mifflin Harcourt Publishing Company. All rights reserved.

Library of Congress Cataloging-in-Publication Data is on file for this title.
LC record is available at http://lccn.loc.gov/2016013264.

Mountaineers Books titles may be purchased for corporate, educational, or other promo-
tional sales, and our authors are available for a wide range of events. For information on
special discounts or booking an author, contact our customer service at 800-553-4453 or
mbooks@mountaineersbooks.org.

 Printed on recycled paper

ISBN (hardcover): 978-1-68051-062-1
ISBN (ebook): 978-1-68051-063-8

To Jim and Arielle Scanlan—
with love and thanks

Hence,
understanding
is always best
and a prudent mind.
Whoever remains
for long here
in this earthly life
will enjoy and endure
more than enough.

—*Beowulf,*
as translated by
Seamus Heaney

{ contents }

One day, seven years after moving to Seattle, I looked up at the fiery-red leaves of a vine maple and knew that the changing leaves meant it was almost the Jewish New Year, Rosh Hashanah, and that soon the salmon would return from the ocean to spawn and die in local creeks. I did not think of the brilliant fall colors of my old home in upstate New York. That was a place from my past. I knew where I was. Now Seattle was my home.

Or so I thought. I wish it were that simple: to know a place just by its species and seasons, and then be able to call it home.

I found home largely through discovering and helping to restore Pacific salmon, a group of creatures that journey from their place of birth, change and grow, and then return home, changed again. *Turning Homeward* offers a glimpse of the theory and practice behind stewardship and restoration, but it's beyond my expertise to offer an analysis of whether decades of restoration can bring back salmon. Similarly, Jewish thought and tradition is far more complicated than what I present, especially surrounding the many interpretations of *tikkun olam*, repairing the world. To learn more about these topics, please go to the acknowledgments and the resources section at the end of the book.

My hope is that *Turning Homeward* contributes to a growing literature of what the historian William Cronon calls "caretaking tales—tales of love and respect, of belonging and responsibility," created when humans are knowledgeable about and committed to the places they care about, whether the faraway wilderness or the nearby neighborhood. Some of my tales are of success, others of failure; some are of lessons learned, others of questions that linger. I hope that each one is a cairn along the trail toward home.

{ cottage lake creek }

Sockeye. Chum. Coho. Chinook. Pink. Steelhead. When I moved to Seattle in the late 1980s, people talked of fish once seen in creeks that had long since been forced under strip malls and parking lots; they spoke of how many salmon they used to catch and how big those sockeye or Chinook were. The anadromous Pacific salmon and trout that had once dominated the rivers and streams of the Pacific Northwest—Washington, Oregon, Idaho, Northern California, British Columbia, and reaching into Alaska—seemed to be everywhere yet nowhere, appearing and then disappearing like an old family ghost, spoken of often but usually in the past tense. Like ghosts fading from human memory, the salmon's return to their ancestral home seemed to become more tenuous with each passing year.

I came to Seattle after having lived for three years in upstate New York's Hudson Valley, where a boulder-strewn creek flowed through my backyard and the Catskill Mountains were close by. For a time, my cottage there was a sanctuary from the stresses and strains of working in a domestic violence program, but it wasn't enough to silence the call for a change echoing through my life. Nature was in abundance outside the small town of Woodstock—but missing were ballet and theater companies, swing dances, neighborhood Chinese restaurants, nearby university classes, Shakespeare in the Park, and many other joys of city life. Seattle had all that and more, yet as much as I enjoyed being back in a city, I found myself longing for nature. And the more I tried to find it in my new home, the more curious I became about salmon.

In 1991, "Pacific Salmon at the Crossroads," a landmark research paper, identified 214 naturally spawning native salmon, steelhead, and sea-run cutthroat trout stocks that faced a high or moderate risk of extinction across California, Oregon, Washington, and Idaho. Forty-one of the at-risk stocks were from Washington State, many from the Puget Sound region, where Seattle is located. Of the eighteen stocks the study cited as "presumed extinct," most were also from my new state. In 1999, Puget Sound Chinook were listed as "threatened" under the federal Endangered Species Act (ESA), as were Hood Canal summer chum, Washington coastal and Lake Ozette sockeye, Lower Columbia River Chinook and chum, and Middle Columbia River steelhead. Upper Columbia River spring Chinook were listed as "endangered." That same year, bull trout were listed as threatened across Washington and the rest of their traditional range. By 2007, Puget Sound steelhead joined the threatened list.

Salmon and their relatives, then, are at once part of this place and yet distant from it, which was rather how I felt about my new life in Seattle. When I started to search for salmon, I never imagined they were with me in Seattle or other nearby urban areas.

Perhaps if I had been a native to the area, I would have known that salmon have always swum through the history of Seattle and its environs. But for me, that knowledge would come later, only after I began taking field trips with the local Sierra Club to see the salmon streams still remaining in King County.

Those first trips south and east of Seattle were along a confusing array of highways and side roads, often to places with names I couldn't remember, much less hope to find on a map. It wouldn't have occurred to me to look for nature within urban or suburban areas while I lived in upstate New York. True, Woodstock had creeks within the town, and country roads led to nearby parklands, but whether it was a solitary encounter with another species during a Catskills hike or a car trip to see a mountainside ablaze with fall's gold and crimson leaves, my paradigm was the same: nature was what lived far from me and my daily routines. Yet there I was in mid-October in a Sierra Club carpool weaving its way through the small city of Redmond, home to Microsoft. We drove past upscale housing developments and horse farms before pulling to the side of a two-lane road beside an unmarked blacktop footpath, which could have been easily mistaken for a driveway.

Behind the neatly cut lawns and multicar garages, flowing through a wild riot of sword fern, lichen-encrusted alder, dense stands of salmonberry, and the ubiquitous Himalayan blackberry, was Cottage Lake Creek, spanned by a rain-battered wooden footbridge. Just a few feet below the bridge, the water was thick with pairs of mating sockeye darting back and forth, nipping the tails and fins of intruders to keep them from their precious redds, the gravel sites for their egg nests.

The sockeye's journey up Bear Creek and then to its tributary, Cottage Lake Creek, was part of an ancient, tattered homecoming of salmon returning from the ocean to mate, and not long afterward, to die, in the same creeks where they were born. (Steelhead and other trout follow a different course, in that not all die after spawning; some may migrate back to the ocean and then return to spawn again.) Having long bridged river to ocean, salmon also link the urban to the wild.

The sockeye had lost the sleek silvery fitness of their ocean phase. Now in mating colors, their bodies were crimson and gleaming in the swift, clear water. The deep green of their heads appeared almost pagan. The males seemed humpbacked; their snouts descended into hooks. Sockeye pressed their bodies close to their mates, their tails quivering in rapid, intense bursts. It seemed absurd that I could hear—cutting through the suburban Sunday sounds of barking dogs and pounding hammers—the sharp, slapping noises of a female salmon lying flat against the creek bed, her crimson body arching out of the shallow water, her tail thumping in determined flaps as she carved a redd into the gravel. In the last, fierce instincts of their lives, the sockeye lunged for deeper water or slashed at nearby fish. The fins of most of the sockeye were pale, and their bodies were dotted with a patchwork of white fungus, which heralded their deaths.

I leaned on the footbridge railing. I stared at the sockeye. I had a strange feeling of awe and incomprehension. I was being called to witness. But what was I seeing? The Pacific Northwest, I'd heard it said many times, was anywhere there were salmon. But what were these fish to me? Years later, I would understand that what I saw that day was the creature that would guide me in turning a strange place into a home.

AS A GIRL GROWING UP in the greater New York City suburbs, the only salmon I saw was the neon-pink lox eaten with bagels and cream cheese each Saturday after Temple Zion's Sabbath morning services. Other than the delicious lox, what little I remember of Temple Zion is my father among the men, each wearing a dark suit under his *tallit*, the white prayer shawl, some with blue or black stripes but all with a *tzitzit* fringe in each of the four corners. Sunlight would pour through the stained-glass windows and onto the women's section, where I sat and watched, my older sister nearby and my mother sharing news and gossip with friends. My father and the other men would be swaying and chanting their prayers. Was his faith just a habit? Or was it a sustaining hope despite the increasing tremors and spreading stiffness that even then would have made prayer difficult for him?

A red-haired bookkeeper at a woodworking firm, Malvin Ross wanted nothing more than to rise from his Naugahyde recliner, walk into a room, hug his daughters, talk and laugh with friends, and maybe drive to work or an occasional movie. All this, and more, was stolen from him, and he was left with uncontrollable tremors and the stiffening of his muscles, as if his skin had turned to stone. I was two and my sister was six when my father's intermittent tremors were explained with a diagnosis of Parkinson's disease, then and now an incurable disease of the nervous system.

Decades later, after my mother had died, I would find crammed in the end tables and cabinets of her Florida home black-and-white photos of a broad-shouldered, muscular man laughing on a swimming dock or rowing a boat across a lake. That man was my father when he was happy, and healthy, and had every reason to be glad to be alive. I never knew that man. I knew a man increasingly forced into immobility, silence, and isolation. I was terrified at the injustice done to him, guilty and angry over my powerlessness to change it, and desperately hopeful that there was something I could do, if not for him, then for the world.

At Temple Zion, I would have been too young to understand the words *tikkun olam*, a term that translates as "repair of the world." In 1950s American Judaism, the term emerged from dormancy as a response to the Holocaust, gained traction in the 1970s and 1980s, and is now embedded in American culture, found in presidential speeches, children's books, and popular movies, where it's understood as a call to action to repair the world's ills. When I was a young woman exploring Judaism and social change movements, the only interpretation of *tikkun olam* I heard was this contemporary one.

It would be decades before I would discover that the term is a centuries-old one in Judaism, with many different meanings at many different times, and with sources in prayer, where it's a call for humanity to live united under God; in Jewish legal thought, where it's invoked to balance competing claims in a way that defuses conflicts and stabilizes the social order; and in mysticism, where spiritual practices are the means for bringing together the shards of divine light scattered throughout the world. Scholars, laypeople, and activists have debated what *tikkun olam* is and isn't; entire books have been written on what it should or shouldn't be. Some of the contention arises from the term itself. Legal historian Levi Cooper notes that *tikkun* comes from a Hebrew root that connotes the related but subtly different terms of "straightening, repairing, [and] refashioning" while the many meanings of *olam* have ranged from the allied yet distinct concepts of community, society, and world, even universe, and eternity.

Some regard interpreting *tikkun olam* as a call to repair-focused actions to be at the heart of the religion; others believe this modern definition narrows our understanding of *tikkun olam* and is all too often used to justify any actions or beliefs the term's speaker thinks are right, which many times default to left-of-center politics. Perhaps this recent interpretation of *tikkun olam* will hold its ground and root firmly in the upcoming generations and centuries; perhaps it won't. I can only say with certainly that wherever I was when I first heard the words *tikkun olam* I know it expressed not just my despair, that seemingly unbridgeable schism between what is and what could be, but also my hope that meaningful action was possible in a world torn asunder. Yet this contemporary interpretation of *tikkun olam* is not strongly associated with the traditional Judaism of my father, who sought meaning or simply mercy.

I can still remember my family's weekly Shabbat, the candles glowing, my father in his *yarmulke* and *tallit*, the wine and challah on our white-and-yellow Formica kitchen table. I can remember the stiffness of our best clothes, which we wore for Rosh Hashanah and Yom Kippur. Even as a young girl, I believe I would have recognized in the words *tikkun olam* the desperate impulse to repair a broken world, though I would spend my adulthood struggling to understand how to turn that impulse into effective action. I would have been too young to understand that the call to repair was not unique to being Jewish but rather a response that can be felt by all people, especially now, when facing a world of so many harms. When I was a child, though, all I knew was that the world was shattered, again and again, into ever-smaller pieces, as my father became increasingly destroyed by Parkinson's disease.

Perhaps it was living so early and close to one wound that opened my eyes to so many other wounds in the world. And it was a world filled with wounds; wherever I looked, that was all I could see.

I left my upstate New York cottage for good one fall not long after my father died. Grown by then and long out of college, I had spent the previous decade as an activist in the nuclear disarmament movement and working in the nonprofit sector, mainly with emergency shelters and domestic violence programs. As a project director at a statewide coalition of battered women's programs, I answered hotline calls and listened to women talk of being beaten, burned, stabbed, raped, and maimed; I tallied monthly data on the number of individuals forced from their homes due to violence; I tracked legislation about orders of protection, batterers' programs, and funding for shelters. I did all of that and more. But for every woman or family who broke free (and many did), day after day, week after week, month after month, there was the next call, the next monthly tally of beatings and emergency shelter stays, the next crisis of desperate people, and the next, and the next, and the next, with no hope of a different future.

I did that for three years. I was exhausted. I quit my job, loaded up my silver Toyota Tercel 4WD, and drove westward with the inchoate hope of a new life in a new place. September's warm days stretched to weeks as I drove in solitude across the Midwest's open fields, crossed the Continental Divide at the Eisenhower Tunnel in Colorado, and traversed the Southwest's red-and-gold landscape. I had never before seen such an expanse of land and sky, opening wherever I looked. In late September, driving north along the California coast, I stopped on a whim at the state park at Point Lobos. Sunlight shone on the Pacific Ocean, sea otters rolled in the kelp, and an unexpected epiphany changed my life: the world was worth saving for its beauty, for its abundance of life.

There was one problem. I had no idea how to begin, certainly not in Seattle, where I would be a newcomer.

I DROVE MY WAY NORTH, reaching Seattle a few weeks later. My reasons for settling there were based more on what I knew I *didn't* want than on a vision for my future. I didn't want to be anywhere near my life in New York. My best friend from high school had settled in San Francisco, as had a postcollege housemate. But I had no desire to go across the country only to walk into a bookstore or restaurant and find someone who remembered me from another time, another place, and thought she knew everything about me. Besides, didn't everyone head off to California?

I had spent a few afternoons at a public library, researching census and other data on different West Coast cities, and discovered that Seattle had colleges and universities (meaning an active cultural life), had a strong nonprofit community (meaning work to be found), was near open water (a relief after landlocked upstate New York), had good demographics in my age group, and I knew no one there. That made Seattle the perfect tabula rasa for my own version of "Go West, young woman!"

My first year there was a series of short-term shared rentals, starting with a married couple enmeshed in debating adoption or divorce. I moved into their house in the Madrona neighborhood in October and thought it dreary until I realized the problem wasn't the tension in the house as much as the world outside, where the sky was drizzly for days, the rare sunlight murky in a grey sky. At first, I discovered Seattle by foot at night, knocking on doors to raise money for a local nonprofit in my stint as one of Seattle's ubiquitous corps of canvassers. Sunday through Thursday, I gathered in the late afternoon with a crew of budding political organizers, a prostitute worried about the state of the world, artists and musicians whose real work was elsewhere and low-paying, and newcomers like me who needed a paycheck while saving the daytime hours for searching for a real job. We piled into vans, drove to targeted neighborhoods, passed out street maps and donor lists, rang doorbells, handed a petition to whoever opened their door, and started a spiel that ended as soon as the person's pen stopped moving on the page and it was time for the fifty-dollar membership ask, and dickered down from there.

Sometime during my first Seattle winter, I took my down jackets and hooded parkas, which I'd carefully packed in the Toyota upon leaving New York, and hauled them off to Goodwill. Back East, people talked of Duofold long johns and Icelandic wool sweaters the way in Seattle people invoked Gore-Tex and fleece. I learned to wear those new clothes on the days I spent exploring Seattle. *I'll head out tomorrow*, I'd think during those first weeks when looking out the window, and it was a while before I understood what my housemates kept saying, that fall through spring, the rain wasn't going to stop tomorrow.

And so in those first years, I knew little of Seattle's salmon or other natural wonders. What I did know, and had known even as a child, was that the lox I ate after temple services was salmon, a fish that came from the Pacific Northwest, a fish that was identified with the place. Even now, it seems odd that as a child, I'd never heard of the Atlantic salmon that once dominated the rivers and streams of New England and the North Atlantic, though that was likely the source of my wonderful New York lox. Yet even on the other side of the continent, I had heard stories of Pacific coast rivers that were so thick with salmon that a person could walk across their backs from one side to the other.

What I hadn't heard was that when the earliest European and later American settlers and fur traders came to the Pacific Northwest, they followed the example of indigenous people and used salmon as a subsistence food source. David Montgomery's *King of Fish* describes how even into the mid-1800s, pioneers found that the salmon in the region were too abundant to have commercial value; settlers hauled spawning salmon out of rivers as fertilizer for their fields or food for farm animals. Attention turned toward Pacific salmon, Montgomery says, at the same time the once-massive returns of Atlantic salmon became so overfished as to retreat toward memory or a story from long ago. Nearly a century and a half later, I can't quite imagine nature so abundant or a place so large as to hold millions of fish swimming upriver.

What turned Pacific salmon from abundance to scarcity was, in part, canning. Salmon could be caught, preserved, shipped back East, and even shipped across oceans, and then be stored for weeks, months, or years, eaten whenever desired. No longer were the fish merely another force of nature. Now the salmon were a valuable commodity, one that could make or break a person's fortune.

From the mid-1800s onward, commercial fisheries, canneries, recreational fishing, and other industries built up around the annual return of the salmon. The all-too-common strategy was to take as many of the returning fish as possible, leaving too few salmon to spawn in rivers and streams. In another publication, Montgomery gives the fishing harvest levels for Puget Sound Chinook, steelhead, and coho as ranging from a low of 60 percent to a high of 90 percent. And those numbers aren't even from the peak of salmon harvesting that occurred from roughly the late nineteenth century into the early twentieth century. Those were the harvests from the 1970s through the 1990s, just prior to the endangered species listings.

In contrast, traditionally salmon have meant food and spiritual sustenance, as well as currency and many other things, to Pacific Northwest Native Americans. As the historian Joseph Taylor notes, traditional Native American fishing techniques, ranging from weirs that blocked salmon passage to net fishing, basket traps, and other methods, were effective enough that they could have removed large numbers of returning salmon, and concludes: ". . . That the Indians did not overfish despite heavy consumption suggests that they practiced some form of restraint . . . Dependence on salmon created complicated forms of respect."

One way of expressing that respect was in a common story found across Pacific Northwest tribes that the returning salmon are not simply fish but are actually the Salmon People, supernatural beings who live in undersea villages. Every year, the Salmon People take the form of fish and make of themselves a great sacrifice, one that feeds us humans here on land. Many Pacific Northwest Native

American cultures treated the first salmon caught as an honored guest, greeting it with sacramental songs and processions, a special feast of its flesh, and, in many areas, a ritual return of its bones to the sea. If the first salmon was given its due, it would tell the rest of the Salmon People, who would then return out of appreciation for the respect and courtesy shown them. First salmon rituals, together with other practices that moderated harvest levels, helped put a limit on Native American salmon fishing, ensuring that strong numbers of salmon returned yearly.

TWISTING WEAKLY in the thick mud, half out of the shallow water, a male sockeye struggled to make his way back to Cottage Lake Creek. The fish had swum underneath the partially raised roots of a cedar and wound up, not in a part of the creek thick with females, but in a tiny mud puddle. He had lost the genetic race. None of the sockeye had eaten since they left the ocean weeks before to make their way upstream to where they were born. Their sole drive was to reproduce, and here was this male—literally and figuratively—stuck in the mud. One of the men on the Sierra Club field trip waded into the black mud, grabbed the struggling sockeye, and tossed it back into the creek. A brief, heated discussion on the ethics of interfering with natural selection ensued, but it ended when someone said, "We can't afford to lose a single one."

Bear Creek and Cottage Lake Creek are tributaries of the Sammamish River, and the sockeye in these streams belong to an independent, naturally spawning population. Although the origin of Bear Creek and Cottage Lake Creek sockeye (formally part of the Lake Washington and Sammamish Tributaries stock, which includes sockeye spawning in Issaquah Creek and other tributaries to Lake Sammamish and the Sammamish River) isn't known, some genetic analyses have shown these fish to be substantially of native origin, whereas other sockeye in the Lake Washington system have been shown to be primarily descended from hatchery fish. The Bear Creek and Cottage Lake Creek sockeye have a fairly consistent pattern of high numbers of sockeye in one year alternating with low numbers returning to spawn the next year. While sockeye numbers were strong in the years I first encountered Cottage Lake Creek (they have since dropped significantly), the fish I saw were nonetheless remarkable survivors against staggering odds. Despite their dwindling numbers, salmon have retained their eerie genetic determination to return. They are, paradoxically, wanderers bonded to home.

For all salmon, whether from Cottage Lake Creek or any other Pacific Northwest waterway, its first home is where it developed as a quivering embryo amid gravel and cold water flowing like wind between stones, the place where it changed to an alevin, a hatchling gaining nourishment from an external yolk sac, and later, as a thin silvery fry, wriggled between the gravel into its natal stream's swift water. Depending on the species, home for a young salmon can be a tributary or stream, a side channel of a large river, an estuary, a lake, for sockeye, or salt water, for chum and pink. (Pink salmon migrate to sea shortly after emerging from the gravel, while chum may go directly downstream or stay in their natal creeks for a few days or weeks.)

Once they head downstream, the salmons' new home becomes nearshore areas, ideally productive and unpolluted estuaries, where as smolts, salmon make complex biological transitions from freshwater to salt water. From there, home then becomes a marine environment where they will spend years feeding in the ocean and growing in strength and size. As adults, the salmon return to estuaries and readjust to freshwater. Last but not least, home becomes the rivers and creeks where salmon will start their upstream migration toward spawning areas. A small number will explore and colonize new river and stream systems, but most will return to the same place their unknown parents sought, spawned, and died.

Regardless of where they mate and die, salmon need rivers and streams offering an open route from freshwater to the ocean and back. Yet for the last century and a half, salmon have had to swim past commercial, recreational, and tribal fisheries, and then fight their way through estuaries clogged with factories, urban development, and industrial ports, only to struggle past or be blocked by dams built for hydroelectric power generation and other uses. They have reached natal creeks and found them run dry from water withdrawal for agricultural irrigation, polluted from widespread use of chemical fertilizers or pesticides, or occupied by striped bass, brook trout, and other introduced species, or in other ways suffer the consequences of logging, grazing, mining, and urban sprawl.

Now salmon face more modern harms, such as the growing number of "farmed" Atlantic, and sometimes Pacific, salmon kept in net pens in local marine waters, which could transmit lethal viruses and parasites, or lead to Atlantic salmon "escapees" that could potentially establish self-sustaining populations that might displace Pacific salmon from freshwater habitat. Also of concern is climate change, which is limiting mountain snowpacks and, with it, the availability of freshwater for river systems. Instead of returning to high, cold streams and rivers, salmon are increasingly returning to waterways that are dry from drought or where the instream water temperature is lethally hot.

Since the late 1800s and through the twentieth century, hatcheries have been the technological fix that was supposed to replace the dwindling salmon. What really happened, though, was that, all too often, releasing large numbers of hatchery fish obscured the declining numbers of wild salmon. High numbers of hatchery fish, in turn, often led to fishing quotas that could only be met by producing more and more hatchery fish that often outcompeted wild fish struggling for freshwater food and habitat.

Bruce Brown's remarkable *Mountain in the Clouds: A Search for the Wild Salmon*, James Lichatowich's *Salmon Without Rivers*, Matthew Klingle's *Emerald City: An Environmental History of Seattle*, Joseph Taylor's *Making Salmon*, and many other scholarly and journalistic investigations show that with the destruction and possible restoration of salmon, an already-complex history of economic desires at odds with eco-logical systems is interwoven with thorny, sometimes violent, and enduring clashes of culture, race, class, and ethics of place. Suffice it to say that by the time I first saw Cottage Lake Creek's sock-eye, salmon had already disappeared from 40 percent of their traditional breeding ranges in Washington, Oregon, Idaho, and Northern California.

WHEN MY TIME with the married couple in Madrona ended (they chose adoption, by the way, and are still married), I moved into a University District house with a musician from Colorado and a missionary-turned-Marxist just back from the Philippines. Long since wearied of canvassing, I returned from yet another job interview, climbed the narrow stairs to my attic room, and sat cross-legged on the beige shag rug, because the slanted roof made standing difficult. It wasn't just the tears in my eyes that made it hard to look out the tiny window and remember whether I was looking westward at the Olympic Mountains or seeing the Cas-cades to the east. Whether it was networking or job interviewing, the questions I couldn't answer were never about my skills: "Isn't Seattle just too small and unsophisticated for someone from New York?" "Will you be staying long in Seattle?" "Why did you come here again?" Lurking under those questions was an unspoken one: *Seattle really isn't your home, is it?*

It didn't help that I'd mispronounced Puget Sound, saying "pooh-get" rather than "pew-jet." The evergreen trees, I realized, were worthy of the name, for they stood green year-round against a sky that should have been blue but was grey. I couldn't understand why drip coffee was hard to find but lattes, espressos, and Americanos (what those were I didn't know) were everywhere. In ways I could taste but not explain, the stir-fried rice in Seattle's International District was different from the Chinese food I'd had in New York, where I still had longtime friends, former colleagues, and other roots of connection and community that made a home.

For months now, home had been where I happened to have my bed, my clothes, my books, my notebooks. What if the people asking those questions at job interviews (and so many other places too) were right? What if I didn't belong here and never would? Yet I wanted a new life and a meaningful place for myself in Seattle. And I knew home wasn't to be found back East. I couldn't have said what home was, exactly, or where it was to be found in Seattle. I only knew I had crossed a continent to get to this place, and I wasn't going to reverse that trip. I cried for a while longer and then made another call, and another, and many others after that, and went out on another interview, and another, and many others after that, and eventually found work with a small nonprofit, which led to yet another rental situation.

Regardless of where I lived, fall was my favorite time of year, a season of abundance and harvest poised between summer's joyous bounty and winter's long, dark gestation. The Jewish holidays were a thread woven across time and landscapes. Fall brought the High Holy Days of Rosh Hashanah and Yom Kippur. As a young girl, I thought the High Holy Days were simply the ten-day period between the New Year and the Day of Atonement. As I grew older, though, I learned that the first month of the Jewish calendar is in the spring, when Passover occurs, which commemorates the liberation of the Jews from slavery in Egypt. In the seventh month of the year will come Rosh Hashanah, which is when the year begins, and then comes Yom Kippur, a time for renewal and repair, followed soon after by the festival of Sukkot, a celebration of the fall harvest and what some interpret as the coming to fruition of the joy and fulfillment that is the culmination of the High Holy Days. Immediately after Sukkot comes Simchat Torah, marking that the yearlong reading of the Torah has come to an end, and it's time to dance with the scrolls and begin reading anew. Two months after that will come Hanukkah, a midwinter celebration of liberation, and then the holiday cycle begins a slow turn toward spring.

Happening midway through the year, the High Holy Days and the month preceding them are a time dedicated to study and self-examination. In the liberal Jewish circles in which I've traveled, from Rosh Hashanah to Yom Kippur we are called to *teshuvah* (turning and returning), *tefillah* (transformative prayer), *tzedakah* (wisely considered charity but perhaps more accurately the obligation to treat others justly), and *tikkun* (repair), which for me is the heartbeat of the High Holy Days. For woven throughout these optimistic days of prayer and ritual is a striving for renewal and repair to the damage in our hearts, our communities, our relationship to whatever is believed to be the transformative force coursing through existence. Deeds are scrutinized, prayers made, apologies offered, forgiveness given. But more importantly to me, actions are taken to repair the harms done, with renewal celebrated with round loaves of challah and apples dipped in honey at Rosh Hashanah, and a communal meal to break the Yom Kippur fast.

While there are variations, most Western Washington salmon runs return in the fall and early winter, before offspring develop in the gravel and then emerge in the spring. Many years, the return of the salmon coincides with the High Holy Days and Sukkot, and beyond to Hanukkah, a joining of past, present, and future that fits the season's spiritual character as one cycle ends in a renewed round of life.

I returned to Cottage Lake Creek often during the fall I first discovered it and for many falls to come. One Sunday afternoon, I watched as a blonde girl of seven or eight ran up the paved trail to the creek's footbridge. She was pulling her older sister and grand-mother in her wake. At the sound of footsteps, several sockeye darted into the shadows under the bridge.

"Phew! Stinky!" she squealed, holding her nose at the smell of the carcasses that were beginning to line the muddy banks. That rotting smell was the sign of a healthy Pacific Northwest stream, one still able to support salmon.

"Here comes another family!" the girl yelled, interrupting her dark-haired older sister's explanation of how far the salmon travel to reach the creek. I looked at the water, expecting to see two sock-eye working their way upstream. Instead, another human family, fuzzy in their blue fleece jackets, joined us at the footbridge. A father stood near his son, both wearing Mariners baseball caps, and pointed out the humpbacked males.

"It's covered with ice!" yelled the young boy, interrupting his father to point to a carcass in the mud.

"It's not ice. It's fungus. The fish are decomposing," the father said, slowly and carefully stressing each syllable as he gave his son a new word. "De-com-pos-ing. The fish are dead. Their bodies are rotting away."

Most people see salmon only at the end of a complicated life.

The sockeye that will hatch out in the spring will soon leave Cottage Lake Creek, perhaps on the very night they twist and turn out of the gravel, and typically spend a year feeding and growing in Lake Sammamish or Lake Washington, where they will stay before making their way downstream. Once at sea, Pacific Northwest sockeye swim in a great spiral dance northward along the Pacific coast, up to Alaska, veering west toward the Aleutians. From there, the sockeye will turn again, this time south and east. This maritime waltz usually lasts two or three years, but can last as long as four, and carries the sockeye thousands of miles from where they began.

Despite their brief sojourn in Cottage Lake Creek, these sockeye knew this area better than I did. The map I used to get there showed streets and intersections, highway entrances, and city limits, not watersheds, drainages, or nesting sites. Another terrain, I began to realize, was present alongside the industrial one. Urban animals had their own haunts and routes that were hidden, or simply unnoticed, alongside the human roads leading to soccer fields and pizza joints, or the concrete trails bisecting suburban housing developments. Habitat, I was learning, is never simply destroyed. It is re-created in ways that express our values and imagination. It is alive with creatures, whether or not we bother to see them.

GRADUALLY, I HEARD ABOUT salmon restoration projects along streams in Seattle and other communities. I got my name on mailing lists, attended trainings, and started volunteering at local sites. As my time in urban and suburban nature increased, I began to notice and learn about other species, from birds to bees to turtles. From those early volunteer opportunities would come a long-standing engagement as a citizen scientist, who observes a part of the local ecosystem—when flowers bud or migratory birds appear, for example—and relays that on-the-ground observational data to professional researchers to help answer scientific questions, often about environmental conservation. In my case, I was a salmon monitor, watching for the number and species of salmon returning to local streams.

My monitoring sites over the years varied, but Cottage Lake Creek remained my favorite. Walking the footpath flanked by big-leaf maple and lichen-covered alder quieted nagging thoughts of clients, schedules, and deadlines. Cottage Lake Creek was a lush green refuge of salmonberry, old cedar trees, and other conifers, where the main sounds were birds and the thump of salmon digging redds.

One weekend, as I counted fish in the creek, a middle-aged woman ran up to me. She had shoulder-length streaked-blonde hair and wore tight-fitting black jeans with a matching jacket. Seeing me with a clipboard left many people thinking I worked for the county, and I often heard complaints about neighborhood life. I could tell this woman wasn't a native to the area: she smiled, started a conversation, and assumed a stranger would reply. That marked her as an outsider, like me.

"Wait 'til you hear what happened to my son!" exclaimed the woman. "Not a week ago, my son—he's fourteen—and his friend sneaked out of the house. It must have been right around midnight, maybe later, and they headed right to the creek, and what do they see? A huge creature, at least seven feet tall, all dark and hairy and looking just like a man, and it stood up and raised its arms practically up to the trees and roared. It was Sasquatch!"

Sasquatch, a.k.a. Bigfoot, is the Pacific Northwest's version of the Himalayan yeti, an ape-man of the woods—whose existence has never been proven, but who is quite alive in stories, folktales, and urban legends.

"Maybe it was a black bear," I naively suggested. "There are a number of parks and greenbelts that would make travel corridors, there are berries along the creek, fish for food—"

"A bear!" The woman reared back. "There are no wild animals in our neighborhood. It was Sasquatch!"

I don't know if Sasquatch exists, but I knew without question that there was wildlife in the neighborhood. Black bears had been spotted in the area. I had seen great blue herons at the creek and had heard that river otters sometimes came to eat the salmon or scavenge their spawned-out carcasses. And surely, deer moved through the large landscaped yards. These and so many other creatures were all part of the woman's home, even if secret from her.

ONE WEEKEND, shortly after I had discovered Cottage Lake Creek, a light rain was falling with the twilight when I returned to the stream. Walking down the slick blacktop path, I jumped as a muffled boom greeted my footsteps. A great blue heron emerged from the tree cover and wheeled its sinuous body over the creek, its blue-grey wings slapping the darkening sky. The heron flew into a brisk evening air rich with smells raised by the afternoon rains. Cutting through the thick aroma of fertile earth was a sharp smell of sweetness gone too far, lost and turning past ripeness into something bitter, pungent, and decaying.

I counted seventeen sockeye salmon carcasses belly-up and twisted. The bodies of some were a fading pink. Others had their skins pulled back to expose flesh and fragile vertebrae. Their bodies seemed to bubble with algae, and their mouths gaped open, filled with fallen leaves.

A Chinook was also in the creek, so still that I thought it was recently dead, until I saw the faint movement of its jaw. Another salmon, a male sockeye with a humped back, undulated slowly through this maze of death. I couldn't help but wonder what, if anything, it made of the dead bodies of its brethren as it searched for a late-arriving female with eggs to lay.

Yet, Cottage Lake Creek was filled with living fish: tiny embryos growing amid the oxygen-rich gravel of the streambed in the creek's dark, rain-swollen waters. By the following spring, when they hatched out as alevins, there would be no sign of their parents other than a vast inheritance of genetic wisdom that would guide them to hide in downed wood, to follow the creek to a lake and then out to sea, to school past the waiting jaws of orcas and harbor seals, to feed and grow, and then one day, to start their way back home.

Standing in the deepening twilight, surrounded by Cottage Lake Creek's fragile wildness, I was struck by the salmon's fierceness in claiming their place regardless of all we've done to this land and its waterways. Fish are strange creatures, slippery, quick, and submerged from view, living in depths I cannot see. Before moving to Seattle, I had never concerned myself with the comings and goings of fish. By now, I had learned to say "turn east" or "west" and not "left" or "right" when giving directions. I had finally accepted I'd never find a real pizza or bagel *anywhere.* I had steady work, stable housing, and friends, all of whom had come to Seattle from somewhere else. The externals of home were falling into place. Yet looking at the sockeye, I had a nagging question: What did it mean to live in this place we shared?

There's nothing like a good question to guide you through a day's growing darkness, through the weeks and seasons and years of your life. The salmon needed neither questions nor answers. Where a few weekends before, the creek was filled with sockeye, tense and protective of their redds, there was now only a solitary pair. Their crimson bodies shone in the darkening light. They sidled next to one another, quivering, undulating over each other's bodies. The female slapped the creek bed with her tail as she dug her redd. They continued with their courtship and nest building, oblivious to the deaths around them, unconcerned with their fate.

{ east king county }

We were salvaging vine maple at this site, and cascara, Indian plum, ocean spray. Also any conifer we could find: western redcedar, Douglas fir, western hemlock. All are native flora often found along Pacific Northwest streams and waterways. By morning's end, thousands of shrubs and seedlings, placed in burlap bags, would fill a rented moving truck. Thousands more would be left behind. The county organizes plant salvages when local forests are set to become housing developments, strip malls, or highways. The flora we were digging up would be replanted along streams, wetlands, and estuaries, many of which were salmon restoration sites.

Was I saving this forest? Or was I just another hand cutting it down?

This site was called Valley Green. Or perhaps it was The Gardens. It's hard to tell one residential development from another. The nostalgic names belie the landscapes they create. A mud path from the forest had been widened to become a rain-slick asphalt road, twisting and curling through unmarked culs-de-sac. There were cleared plots of rock and grey dirt, white pipes, and neon-yellow earth-moving machines. Stuck in the dirt were white posts printed with black block letters that said "Storm Sewer Water."

The model home was open for display. It was a beige house with a tan roof, four windows to each side, and a two-car garage. I tried to imagine what this land would look like with two hundred, three hundred, four hundred beige houses—all with clipped lawns—standing side by side. Weeks or months or years later, I might drive past The Gardens, Valley Green, or other suburban developments, with names like Meadowdale or Emerald Creek, and would never recognize the land where I had spent Saturday mornings filling burlap bags with big-leaf maple, thimbleberry, sword fern, salmonberry, snowberry, and more.

The county ecologist overseeing the several dozen volunteers was standing nearby. She was dressed for rain, of course. She wore boots and dirty jeans, and her white-streaked black hair was sheltered under a wide-brimmed khaki hat.

"How much is coming down?" I asked her.

We looked toward the forest. The woods were a labyrinth of salal, sword fern, Oregon grape, red huckleberry, and alder. Tight trillium buds were just rising from the dark, rain-soft earth. These were the few I had learned to notice and identify in this green blur of a forest. Growing beside them were so many more I had not yet come to know. It struck me: I'd lived in Seattle for nearly ten years, yet I was still so new to this region. And there I was learning to identify the flora by salvaging it.

I heard the trill of wrens. I heard the soft thud of shovels.

"All of it," the ecologist said, shrugging. "All of it."

"HOPE IS THE THING with feathers / that perches in the soul," wrote Emily Dickinson. And in these woods, there were small hopes. Bumble bee queens, pregnant and waiting for spring, were somewhere hidden in the cracks of a nurse log or in the earth beneath a tangle of winter's golden grass. A bird, perhaps twice as big as my thumb, flitted through the alder trees. I looked for field marks to identify it. I tried to remember the slides I'd seen at Seattle Audubon classes. Red-breasted nuthatch, most likely, I decided. A Pacific wren foraged under curling fronds of sword fern. That bird I knew. *Chit, chit, chit,* it called, so close I could see its pale eyebrows. Dark-eyed juncos with plumage looking like a monk's brown cowl darted amid the roots and fallen leaves. At the edge of my sight, a hawk flew into an alder stand. A Cooper's hawk, or perhaps a sharp-shinned hawk. There was a rustling in the fallen leaves, then silence. If woods like these kept coming down, would I ever have a chance to learn one accipiter from another?

When I was young, I wanted to save the world. I thought I could do that by organizing and boycotting and marching and leafleting and demonstrating against the big issues: nuclear proliferation; violence against women; so many other avoidable injustices of our time. I value that activism for what it changed in other people's lives, and for what I learned from it; I trust it made a difference, however slight. I would do it again if necessary.

Now that I'm older, I still want to save the world. But time is costly. Passion more so. I no longer want to determine my actions and define my life by what I oppose. I want to act and live here in this world with what I love, simply and solely because I am coming to love it.

THROUGHOUT THE CENTURIES, sages from various schools of thought have talked of the *anima mundi*, the soul of the world. Annie Dillard, in *For the Time Being*, quotes Rabbi Menachem Nahum of Chernobyl, presumably the renowned eighteenth-century Hasidic rabbi, as saying "All being itself is derived from God and the presence of the Creator is in each created thing." Dillard refers to this as the theological notion of *pan-entheism* (she added the hyphen to distinguish it from *pantheism*), a view she describes as God being seen as "immanent in everything" and where "everything is simultaneously in God, within God the transcendent. There is a divine, not just bushes."

Is there a God? I don't know. Is there evolution? Yes. Regardless of what caused life, are we separate souls lonely, disjointed, longing for salvation? I hope not. Are we a community, a shared life beyond our small knowledge? I hope so.

I FOUND A BUSH of barren limbs. Its branches ended in tight central buds surrounded by hornlike sprouts. Cascara. Its bitter silvery-grey bark was once used as a laxative. I dug the cascara out from under an alder stand and placed it in a moist burlap sack printed with the words *Volcanbara Café—Coffee Peabody*. Even in these woods, I'm not far from Seattle's coffee-focused culture of gourmet microroasters and coffee shops on every street.

A conifer seedling was rooted under the shiny leaves of a salal. Its pencil-thin trunk was no higher than my knee. Short dark-green needles were scattered on its branches in a hectic, feathery pattern. I checked my field guide and then the notes I took during the volunteer training. Two thin lines on the underside of each needle were what helped me identify it—western hemlock.

Jim Pojar and Andy MacKinnon's *Plants of the Pacific Northwest Coast*, a classic field guide and my main reference for all matters botanical, describes how for the indigenous Northwest tribes the wood of western hemlock became hooks for catching halibut; festive bowls or everyday baskets; roasting spits; spear shafts; elderberry-picking hooks; and much more. Its branches made bedding, its pitch made liniment and poultices, and its bark was brewed with cascara and red alder to make a tea to stop internal bleeding.

Fragile roots, now shorn of earth, fluttered in the breeze. The seedling went into the burlap sack along with moist leaves and fragrant black earth.

I found what I thought was vine maple by its maroon bark and its pairs of buds on each twig tip. I checked my salvage list and training notes for the next plant to find, and started looking for Indian plum blossoms in the dull March rain, but I couldn't find any. Instead, I found what I thought was red huckleberry, its thin green branches looking to me like an intricate notched fan. It was not on the salvage list. I left it behind.

TANGLE BILLIONS OF YEARS to make a forest. Add wind, rain, the pull of the moon, and the retreat of ice and snow. Throw in the price of lumber. Add bits of moss, feathers, and insect cocoons lining the nests of black-capped chickadees. Throw in the price of land. Add sun glinting on a bee's wing, a spotted towhee under salal, my heartbeat, the broken pebbles scraping my shovel—all the mundane parts of life encompassing geological shifts, DNA, random chance, or whatever is the transformative force behind existence.

The forest at this salvage site had been logged at least once over the past century. Stumps slick with moss and rain were scattered between thick hemlock and alder covered with ebony-edged tufts of bone lichen. Logging surged in successive waves during the nineteenth and twentieth centuries, tearing through ancient coastal forests of redwood, pine, spruce, hemlock, cedar, fir, and other native flora, which once stretched from Northern California through Oregon, Washington, British Columbia, and on up to Prince William Sound in Alaska.

By the early 1990s, the remaining scattered, tattered forests were cut for their land more than their trees. Washington State lost some two million acres of forests between 1970 and the early 1990s, with nearly 10 percent replaced by urban, suburban, or agricultural uses.

Between 1970 and 2000, King County's population alone shot upward, as did its suburban and exurban developments. The county tried, but failed, to concentrate high-density growth within designated urban areas. Suburban and exurban lands increased, as did single-family housing. Wild lands and agricultural lands decreased.

The bits and pieces of forest we were salvaging would be replanted at restoration sites in parks and preserves, protected streams, wetlands, estuaries, and greenbelts. These disconnected habitats—that some call "biological islands"—can be particularly sensitive to habitat destruction and other drivers of extinction, such as invasive species that outcompete native species for food and shelter.

Was I saving this forest? Or was I just another hand cutting it down?

I never go back to these places after plant salvages. I want to believe I'm only here to help and not to harm. I want to believe there's been a delay, a reprieve, a saving grace.

MY FRIEND LINDA AND I meditated in forests like these in the early 1990s. I was writing newsletters and grants for an environmental education program during the day and finding my way into networks of dancers, hikers, and writers on evenings and weekends. There I found a few native Seattleites but far more compatriot newcomers like Linda, whom I met at a circle of women writers. Every Monday night, we'd gather, slip off our Rockports and Danskos, and put on Polartec slippers. Amid ficus and stonework, we'd hone our words and stories.

I was just starting to write. Linda had already published an acclaimed book on women and science. We could talk for hours about women, science, and spirit during our drives to parks and trails. Once in the woods, we'd grow quieter and find an old place, if we were lucky, where the fir trees were thick with centuries, and rare streaks of sunlight cut through the shadows. Linda looked for waterfalls or boulders left by retreating glaciers. I looked for western redcedar.

Pojar and MacKinnon quote a Coast Salish belief that redcedar was made by the Great Spirit "in honour of a man who was always helping others." From redcedar came "dugout canoes, house planks and posts . . . bentwood boxes, baskets . . . cradles, coffins . . . fish weirs, spirit whistles," not to mention everything from hats to herring rakes and innumerable other objects at the heart of daily life. Some believed the cedar was so powerful that a person could receive strength by leaning backward against its fibrous bark.

There were times I was lucky and found an old tree pulsing with energy. I would sit amid its tangled roots, my eyes closed and my back against its firm trunk. Sometimes I would feel a subtle shift in the air. A tingling of benevolence. A veil parting.

One day, as we were following a curving path out of a forest, Linda told me what her spiritual teacher had said: "The souls of the trees are leaving Earth."

Trees have souls? I thought.

"Where are they going?" I asked.

"Other places. They can't stand what we're doing. They just can't stay here with us any longer."

HOWARD SCHWARTZ, writing in *Tree of Souls: The Mythology of Judaism*, tells of a tree in Paradise from which souls blossom. There are other stories about trees and souls; Schwartz and others write of Rabbi Isaac Luria, the sixteenth-century mystic, who claimed to see souls in trees, one time seeing souls that failed to repent during their lives and that took shelter in the trees and beseeched him for help. Human souls, I presume. But Schwartz also writes of Jewish stories of trees having souls of their own, and of Rabbi Nachman, the late eighteenth-century Hasidic master, who stopped to sleep one night at an inn, only to wake from nightmares. The rabbi consulted one of his books, where it was written, "Cutting down a tree before its time is the same as killing a soul." The inn had been built of saplings cut before their time; Nachman had dreamed of their murder, the calling of their souls.

WHAT HAPPENS WHEN A TREE DIES? A Douglas fir crashes to the forest floor. Not long afterward fungi and bacteria begin to weaken the wood. Beetles and other insects that bore wood chew through the outer bark, opening a habitat of entryways and tunnels that will be used by mites, centipedes, millipedes, slugs, snails, and a host of other invertebrates. Sloughed bark and rotten wood will become a maze of tunnels and burrows carved by salamanders, shrews, and other vertebrates seeking shelter.

Give it a little more time and the fallen Douglas fir will become a nurse log. Its decay will restore nutrients to the soil; its trunk will offer a new world, where seeds of red huckleberry, western hemlock, western redcedar and other trees can fall, sprout, take root. A western redcedar can live for one thousand years or longer before falling to the forest floor. It can live for centuries after its death as a nurse log for seeds and saplings.

Does a tree have a soul? Does a tree need a soul when it has so much life within it? I can almost hear Linda saying, "Does it have to be either-or? Can't it be both-and?" Every forest is its own resurrection.

A CEDAR SEEDLING grew besides a mossy weaving of alder nurse logs. I turned my shovel to find the place between red-black earth and rock where the blade could cut through. Past the grit I found a tangled net of roots. I felt a tug of resistance. The cedar wouldn't give way easily to my good intentions. Natural selection favors adaptability, but also tenacity, perseverance, and rootedness.

I wanted—I needed—to find that small sharp edge of faith in the power of life to drop seeds, take root, and continue on in unlikely places. I dug deeper. The cedar came up beside a clump of bird's-nest fungus; a drop of rain was in each tiny cup. In my shovel were stones, bits of twigs, the moist umber chips of a long-dead cedar, and the tight ebony curl of an insect—the small life of a place.

{ ellsworth creek }

Each fall, my journeys to see salmon led me farther out of Seattle, to streams beyond Cottage Lake Creek and Bear Creek. Some Saturdays I'd drive hours northward, where coyotes crossed a rain-slicked State Route 20, where horse pastures and dairy farms were next to roadside espresso stands, and where the Skagit River pulsed with eagles gathering to eat the returning salmon. Other days found me wandering a Byzantine snarl of suburban roads and culs-de-sac, where an unmarked foot trail would take me to a stream sheltering a local run. Often all it took was staying alert while driving and spotting the small blue signs with a white fish and the words *This Stream Is in* Your *Care*.

I learned to pull over, walk around a bit, perhaps stay and explore. Sometimes all I had to do was find a city park with a stream flowing through it. Even Seattle, I later learned, had urban salmon streams in its parks, including Longfellow Creek, which later became the site of much of my citizen science activities.

The more I journeyed, the better I understood that I lived in a place woven together by rivers, streams, and salmon. The streams I visited when I went east and crossed Lake Washington, such as Bear Creek and Cottage Lake Creek, are part of the Sammamish River watershed, which are part of the Lake Washington—Cedar River drainage, which is just one part of the Puget Sound region's more than twenty large river systems and tributaries.

An inner geography was taking shape to match the landscape. My first years in Seattle were a disorienting stretch of rain and grey skies from September to May. I waited in vain for the seasons of the Northeast that I knew so well: an autumn of crimson and purple leaves, of brisk winds and bright days that hardened into winter snow gleaming in starlight and air so cold it burned my lungs, only to warm in time with spring roses unfurling to gleam and then slowly wither away as summer's bright sun faded with the coming fall. As I learned to look past Seattle's rain and see the return of the salmon as a sign that a distinct time of year had begun, I became aware of other animal migrations marking my new home. Winter was when red-tailed hawks perched atop highway streetlamps. Spring was when the turtles called red-eared sliders emerged from brumation (akin to hibernation) and sunned on logs along the shores of one of Seattle's busiest parks, Green Lake. It felt like an old-fashioned way of learning about a place, as if I had entered my new home through the back door.

When not exploring Seattle and its environs, I was working in the nonprofit sector. Whether I wore jeans and sandals or black skirts and sensible shoes, the jobs changed every few years but were largely the same mishmash of editing newsletters, writing grants, and other "communications and development" tasks. In some ways, I was the same, too. "You still have your New York accent," said a veteran of my old canvass crew, a Canadian who came to Seattle by way of Chicago, when she saw me for the first time in years while at a meeting of community organizations. She wasn't the only person to point my accent out.

Luckily, I didn't have to fit in to thrive. Seattle respects, even cheers, entrepreneurs, and though it took a while, eventually I launched my own freelance grant writing business. Until then, I was busy volunteering, increasingly on environmental issues, whether by phone-banking voters or organizing fund-raisers. Once, I traveled to Washington, DC, as a citizen advocating for wilderness protection for the Arctic National Wildlife Refuge, a breeding ground for so many of the migratory birds I was coming to know, many of which journeyed through one of my favorite places for exploring urban nature, the Montlake Fill alongside the University of Washington campus.

I knew that political advocacy and legal challenges were critical for salmon recovery. I was grateful that other people were doing that work. For myself, though, I needed something humbler than words or power. I needed to get my hands into this still-strange landscape if I were ever to turn it into one better-known, perhaps even a home.

It was a different way of learning about a place than that of the woman I'd met at Cottage Lake Creek, who had insisted her son had seen Sasquatch alongside their suburban stream. Salmon, like Sasquatch, were also legendary in a sense. As their numbers diminished, they had become more symbols of a place than real creatures living in it. Having a relationship with Sasquatch requires little more than imagination and some adventurous teenage boys. Having a relationship with salmon, I was coming to understand, meant more than visiting streams out of curiosity. I had to earn what I learned from their lives and creeks, and as I did, *tikkun* grew into a deeper exploration of place.

I discovered Hamm Creek, a Duwamish River tributary, by weeding invasive flora and planting native shrubs that would shade and cool the stream water there for juvenile salmon or returning adults. I discovered Honey Creek, part of the East Lake Washington basin, by monitoring it for spawning salmon. To reach it, I'd walk down a road running through a greenbelt of sword fern, Himalayan blackberry, and big-leaf maple, towering conifers entwined with English ivy and morning glory, trashed bicycles, and broken beer bottles in the pale, brittle grass. I saw golden-crowned kinglets and a Cooper's hawk gliding into the lavender twilight, but I never saw any salmon. I can only hope that others had more luck or skill. Cavanaugh Pond, off the Cedar River's main stem and east of Renton, on the other hand, often had a late run of sockeye, which I discovered by removing invasive Himalayan blackberry there. Otherwise, I'd never have thought that behind a trailer park would be a dirt road leading to a river that had one of the strongest sockeye runs in the Lower 48.

At Kelsey Creek and other streams in Bellevue, east of Seattle and across Lake Washington, I helped place incubation tubes in the stream so as to provide coho fertilized eggs with a sheltered environment while they developed into alevins. I can still remember one of the mornings I spent with Bellevue's Stream Team at a stream bend that flowed through a suburban backyard. I had lifted tissue paper off a plastic container filled with thousands of coho eggs floating in iodine-laced water. I reached in and cupped my fingers around orange eggs, each no bigger than my fingernail, perhaps a hundred quivering and translucent in the palms of my hands. It seemed to me that the eggs twitched as if turning skyward in some first, rudimentary glimpse of sunlight. Rain falling on my face, I turned to that same soft light and looked down at the eggs, thinking *I'm holding the watershed in my hands*.

An epiphany without action is just a stray thought. I gritted my teeth and plunged my arm down a corrugated black plastic tube filled with frigid stream water. I forced open my cold-swollen fingers to place the eggs atop a bottom layer of gravel. I pulled my

arm out, grabbed a handful of gravel, and shoved my arm back
into the tube to lay rough stones over the eggs, approximating the
gravel redds dug by female salmon. I pulled out my numb arm.
Another volunteer came forward to lay the next layer of eggs and
gravel. Once filled, the incubation tube was covered with wire
mesh over its open end, and our assortment of fishermen, retir-
ees, and other nature-loving strangers hauled the thirty-pound
tubes into the stream and anchored the ends with rebar, which
we pounded with sledgehammers until secured to the streambed.

The coho in the tubes would have several months to develop in
a sheltered environment, safe from the flash floods, high-pressure
winter flows, and erosion common to urban areas that can scour
out or suffocate redds. Eventually, they would grow into young fish
that would swim out the mesh ends and enter the stream.

The following spring, other volunteers and I returned to pull
the tubes from Kelsey Creek's fast flow, pour water and gravel
onto a blue tarp, and find crawfish, and once a lamprey, amid the
few smashed bits of dead eggs. A kingfisher's shrill, repetitive call
offered paradoxical reassurance: a predator meant there was prey.
Young salmon must be in the creek. And in fact, the tube's hatch-
out rate was high.

Time and again, I would see this coming together of strangers engaged in restoring some small and often overlooked place.
Time and again, my notions of how to save the world expanded
beyond protests and boycotts, citizen lobbying, and picketing to
also include these quieter sustained actions of repair. There was
little time to talk before splitting off to our physical tasks, yet I still
met bearded fish geeks and stout-bellied businessmen, veterans
and vegetarians, Native Americans, recreational and commercial
fishermen and fisherwomen, high school students needing community service credits, and parents and grandparents introducing

their younger children to a world beyond electronic screens. These people weren't activists (although they may have been at other times or for other issues) as much as they were citizens, not in the narrow legal sense, but rather people who knew where they lived and understood the impact of their actions, and who were willing to dedicate their time and energy, hope and heart to a place's future.

Just as the citizens I met were varied, so too were the landscapes these creeks ran through, but all too often the restoration challenges were the same. The more I put my hands into this place where I lived, the more I realized that there was no local harm or local repair or local place that wasn't part of a larger place.

Salmon swam through not just the Pacific Northwest's natural landscapes but its environmental policies and practices. The cheap electricity that lit my apartment came largely from hydropower dams placed along the Skagit River, used by Chinook, sockeye, coho, chum, and pink, as well as steelhead trout and other fish. I'd traveled up to the Gorge Powerhouse, about two hours northeast of Seattle, where vine maple trees blazed red and orange against a grey sky thick with rain; I'd seen stones under the river's clear water, and a hundred or so pink salmon holding steady against the flow, seeming eerily patient, as if they could outlast the hum of electricity in the air, outlast the city and all its lightbulbs and toaster ovens and dryers. But in reality, those fish wouldn't outlast anything without human action on their behalf. Returning home, the least I could do was install compact fluorescent bulbs and turn off lights in empty rooms.

Closer to home, I saw the Hiram M. Chittenden Locks (a.k.a. Ballard Locks) where boats enter concrete and metal compartments filled with water that is raised or lowered from lake to sea level (or the reverse) to allow passage to and from Lake Washington and

Puget Sound. On the Locks' salt water side is Salmon Bay, where the seven-mile-long Lake Washington Ship Canal begins, while on the freshwater side the canal continues, running past marinas, high-tech companies, and the University of Washington, eventually connecting Lake Union to Lake Washington.

Officially opened in 1917 to create direct access to Puget Sound, the Locks were a driver of Seattle's economic development and have seen many changes to facilitate fish passage. During their varying migration times, from roughly late spring and early summer through fall, adult sockeye, coho, threatened steelhead (which migrate in the winter and spring), and threatened Chinook salmon swim past the occasional predatory sea lion or harbor seal; some salmon go through the Locks with boats, while others use the fish ladder to reach freshwater. From there adult salmon make their way to the Lake Washington-Cedar-Sammamish watershed's natal streams and hatcheries. In the spring, young salmon make the reverse trip, journeying past stone breakwaters, concrete docks, and a host of predatory fish with some reaching Puget Sound by going through smolt fumes over the Locks' spillway and others going out alongside ships.

The Cedar River is Seattle's water source and home to a sizable sockeye run. At parks along the Cedar River, I'd heard the cars honking, the mallards quacking, the kids yelling as they raced bikes, and, if I was lucky, I'd heard the sudden splashing of water. I'd seen a dorsal fin brush the air, only to slide underwater as a crimson sockeye glided away. If I was sharing a river's water with a salmon run, I could play my small part by installing water-efficient faucets and using other water-wise practices.

These and other small daily actions may have been about as effective as putting a Band-Aid on a burst artery. But they tethered me to the rhythms of this place. I was learning how to live here.

I was turning homeward, a place where I wanted to see salmon in local creeks. My personal efforts came full circle with professional ones as I increasingly focused my freelance grant writing on raising funds for water trusts and other environmental restoration and education programs.

At first, I thought we could bring back the salmon to their traditional creeks and streams, as if turning back time were as simple as pushing the hands of a clock. What I didn't yet know, and what Kelsey and Longfellow creeks would eventually teach me, is that restoration is never a matter of bringing back the past. And I couldn't silence the nagging question: How much of this was simply to feel as if I belonged here?

My lurching from optimism to cynicism and back felt like just another way I was still a newcomer with much to learn about this place's potential for restoration. (Although I later realized that plenty of the region's longtimers had the same reaction.) Salmon did return to Kelsey Creek and other streams, but success uncovered new failures as returning coho died from toxic stormwater runoff pouring into urban creeks. It would be years before I realized that while much restoration was possible, the scars of the past remain. Ellsworth Creek in southwestern Washington was my first glimpse of genuine possibilities.

I first heard of Ellsworth Creek when I read a local newspaper article about how The Nature Conservancy (TNC) in Washington was raising $20 million to purchase some three hundred acres of old-growth forests growing along the two-and-a-half-mile Ellsworth Creek corridor, as well as some five thousand surrounding acres. That much cash needed all the free publicity it could get, and TNC was organizing a media campaign that included getting local reporters into the watershed. When I read that Ellsworth Creek had a salmon run, I called TNC's Seattle office, and relying on the name of a staff person who attended my synagogue, and on the strength of a few essays I'd published on urban wildlife, I finagled a place on a tour into one of the West Coast's few remaining coastal temperate rain forests.

I carpooled with TNC staff down US Highway 101 into south-western Washington, traveling past Aberdeen, past Artic, past Raymond, past all the tree towns where trucks rumble laden with logs from the Willapa Hills. Trees, logs, and wood had been the coin of this land's realm for more than a century. It was a rough coin now, splintered. Highway 101 curled past Douglas fir tree farms, past a great blue heron in flight, past black cows grazing on tideflats, past the Naselle River, past sunlight striking stumps, and past steam rising off pyramids of logs stacked for shipment out.

We rendezvoused with the cars carrying some newspaper reporters, and Rex Ziak, a lanky photographer, filmmaker, and self-trained historian. Ziak was the son and grandson of loggers and had lived in southwestern Washington his entire life. He was dedicating nearly all his spare time to saving the remaining parcels of old-growth trees. In the early 1990s, he prevented the logging of Teal Slough by the John Hancock insurance company, and he had since struggled to persuade the company to not cut the largest remaining stand of old-growth in southwestern Washington, located on Ells-worth Creek. Ziak eventually contacted TNC about Ellsworth, and that led to its campaign to purchase these thousands of acres.

At Willapa Bay, a one-lane dirt track took our three-car car-avan into the Ellsworth Creek watershed. There, dust rose from an unpaved road, and rocks dented our cars. We stopped short of where an old logging road broke off to stone and dirt. An ankle-high conifer forest sprouted between wheel ruts, and tire tracks cut a red-berry smash of black bear scat.

We were high enough to glimpse the surrounding hills where clear-cuts had left behind trees, limbs, and stumps, now sun-silvered and scattered like bones. The Willapa Hills' coniferous forests had been crossed with logging roads, cut and regrown as monoculture Douglas fir, and cut and regrown again (and possibly again), until less than 1 percent of its original temperate rain forest remained. But along this dirt road was a stand of conifers, and a foot trail that wove between tall trees and led to a boot-cut staircase of squishing mud.

We walked into a green world of eight-hundred-year-old (or older) cedar trees, some thirty feet or more across and burdened with insect galls the size of a Volkswagen Beetle. We had our eyes and notebooks open, and a ready flow of questions. At least the reporters had questions. I was too amazed by what I saw to know what to ask. And so we walked past hemlock grown old and inter-laced. We walked amid rainfall that had tangled in treetops and then slid downward to gleam on a spider's web, or bead along thick strands of bone lichen, ragbag lichen, wolf lichen, or old man's beard clinging to umber bark.

We walked until we found Ellsworth Creek, cutting and curling through the forest. A ribbon of sunlight rode the water. Wild chum salmon darted beneath the radiance. Fast as a ripple. Then gone. The chum were larger than I'd ever seen. The males were fang-jawed. Their bodies were thick and purple-streaked. The females had black lateral lines from tail to gills, signaling their readiness to lay eggs. Chum lack the crimson beauty of sockeye. Chum lack the majesty of Chinook. Chum, or dog salmon, as they're often called, lack the elusiveness of coho. Chum are graceless, perhaps, yet strong-bodied. Persistent. They reminded me of myself, hope-fully making my way into the Pacific Northwest's landscape, with a reason for being here.

A beaver-chewed tree spanned the stream. Chum slithered between its branches, rested against its roots, pushed against the current to reach the gravelly bend, where years earlier they hatched out as alevins, and as fry bonded to a stream they lived in for but a few days before surrendering to the nighttime flow pushing them downstream to Willapa Bay and the Pacific Ocean, north along the coast to British Columbia, and into the Gulf of Alaska. Then they stopped. They changed direction. They swam back. Past Alaska, past British Columbia, into Willapa Bay's estuaries, eventually up Ellsworth Creek, they returned two or three or four years later to mate and die, swimming into a story older than this stream and the land it flows through.

There chum pushed upstream, past a trio of males surrounding a female, past fish listless and covered with golden fungus, past a dead male on a gravel bar, his unseeing eyes staring into sunlight. His head pointed to the stream bank, where a tangle of deadwood bloomed with moss and mushrooms, and dewdrops brimmed over bird's-nest fungus. And in the forest beyond the creek were tree stumps that were left from logging done decades ago—now nurseries for wood sorrel and seedlings of spruce, cedar, red huckleberry, hemlock.

Nothing in nature's resilience excuses past harms or justifies new ones. And if I forgot that and wanted to see only this land's beauty, Rex had more experienced eyes than mine. He pointed out the trenches, as unnaturally straight as a scar line, that were cut into this place to haul out trees, now overgrown with sword fern, deer fern, salal. No matter the roads I took or the streams I explored, it was everywhere to see: this broken world, full of lost spaces, filling its scars with beauty, bursting not with the life that was, but with what could still be.

{ the montlake house }

Tikkun was easy as long as it meant spending an occasional Saturday at a restoration event, volunteering to try and repair what needed to be fixed. There wasn't a creek flowing through my living room. There weren't rotting coho lining the hallways. But repair wasn't so easy when what needed to be fixed was the problem of bumble bees that had invaded my home.

Bees crave light. Once inside my bedroom, they apparently forgot how they had entered, whether through an open sash or a crack in the window frame. Evolution had not prepared them for following summer light back out through glass windows. I watched as fragile wings beat into a black-veined blur as bees tried to fly through my window and back outside to the garden. These were worker bees, after all, each of them a nonreproductive female with one of their main roles being gathering food for the rest of the colony. When each bee finally calmed down, I caught her in a glass cup and released her outside, watching her fly to the orange nasturtiums like an infant kept too long from the breast.

There was a certain noblesse oblige in my actions. If the bees were grateful, they gave no sign. Off they went, without even the proverbial backward glance, to where the hot July days were sending sunlight falling in sharp, shining sheets over the tattered rosebushes and scraggly lawn of a house I rented with three house-mates, all massage therapists who moonlighted as dancers and yoga instructors.

I'd only been living in this house for a few weeks when the bees arrived. I'd answered the massage therapists' ad for another house-mate and moved in because I needed two rooms, a bedroom and a home office in which to launch my business, at a cheap rent. Even better, this close to the 520 bridge, I was a mere fifteen minutes from Cottage Lake Creek (if it wasn't rush hour) and just across a short drawbridge from the Montlake Fill, my favorite wild place in the city.

I didn't release the bees out of a fondness for insects. I tol-erated the spiders spreading their delicate webs in my bathroom corners. They were my allies, eating the flies and whatever else was wandering through my basement rooms. And how could anyone hate butterflies or ladybugs? But it takes an act of sheer intellectual will for me to remember I share a far distant evolutionary ancestor with all the other creeping, crawling creatures I collectively ignore and dismiss as *bugs*.

While I couldn't claim to know a great deal about bees, I did know that the ones hovering about my scented candles, their fuzzy black bodies crowned with a yellow cap and tipped with a gold ring around their tail, were bumble bees. Was it pollinating behav-ior when a bumble bee arched its fuzzy body and rubbed its thin legs over the powdery remains of my incense sticks? What was the function of the translucent droppings the bees left on the red and yellow wax hanging from my brass Hanukkah menorahs? The longer I watched the bumble bees, the more enchanted I became with their short, intricate lives. Unfortunately, they were drop-ping like flies. Losing even part of a day trapped in my bedroom was too long in a life that lasted a few weeks.

At first, there had been just one bee. Then another. And another. Soon there were too many bees. Every morning, I'd pull out the teacup and get as many bees outside as I could. Then I'd cook breakfast and start calling clients for my grant writing business. By midmorning, four, five, sometimes six or more bees would be buzzing, huzzing, hizzing above my shoulders.

And the bees weren't only flying. They were also crawling: across the beige carpet in my office, across the white linoleum in my bathroom (making it impossible for me to step out of the shower without first being sure nothing was moving between the bath mat and my slippers), and—to my horror—across my bed.

Noblesse oblige collapsed before raw survival instinct. The basement's spiders and I could share the same habitat thanks to mutually exclusive niches. The bumble bees were invading my space. I wanted them gone from my life. But I didn't want them killed.

I called the environmentally responsible exterminators. This was the late 1990s when honey bees and bumble bees seemed as ordinary and abundant as flowers. Unbeknownst to most people, several wild bumble bee species were already declining in number and range. By 2006 to 2007, colony collapse disorder would begin to decimate honey bee hives. While possible causes include disease and loss of habitat, the leading culprit has shaped up to be pesticide exposure, even at the common dosages once thought to be nonfatal to bees. The exterminators told me that honey bees could be sold to a beekeeper needing a new hive, but bumble bees were commercially worthless. They produced no honey or anything else that could be sold.

Or at least nothing that could be sold immediately. Bumble bees are worth billions of dollars to North American farmers, if only for their role in pollinating clover, alfalfa, raspberries, apple trees, plum trees, and many other plants. Usually, we think of honey bees when it comes to pollination, but honey bees aren't native to North America, while some forty-five species of bumble bees are.

The bumble bees at the Montlake house were pollinating the ruby-red roses and the purple phlox outside my bedroom window. Where was the money in that? There was only one thing to do with bumble bees.

"We use a spray," the exterminators said.

"What does it do?" I asked, as if I didn't know.

"It's made of chrysanthemums. It won't hurt you at all. Don't worry."

"What does it do to the bees?"

"Kills 'em. Kills 'em dead. But don't worry. It won't hurt you at all."

Bumble bees are cavity nesters, and the exterminators insisted the bees were coming into the house from a hole in the outside walls. Inside the wall must be their nest. But the only holes I found were where my window didn't quite meet the frame. "Could the bees be nesting outside?" I asked the exterminators. "Perhaps wriggling into my bedroom and then forgetting how to wriggle out?"

"Highly unlikely," I was told. So I kept searching for the entry hole. While I didn't find any bees, I did discover a hornet nest hanging from our garage roof. If bees inspired mixed feelings in me, hornets were nothing but gleaming ebony messengers of dread.

Standing in my driveway, I squinted into the bright sun to watch the hornets. My housemates and I must have opened the garage doors countless times not knowing they were there. If the nest continued to grow, we would no longer be able to open the doors without bringing down an insect battle squadron.

Discouraged, I returned to my bedroom, where the bees were buzzing with unfailing persistence against the windowpanes. The summer was blazing hot and as short-lived as the bees. Outside my windows were yellow marigolds with their ruffled petals, pink daisies, ruby-red roses, and ghostly white morning glories encircling the Douglas fir towering over our backyard. The house had been a rental owned by an absentee landlord for a long time before my housemates had moved in. They'd spent their first years there decorating the house with futons and African wood carvings, and putting cactus and dieffenbachia plants near the many windows, but caring for a garden and its flowers wasn't part of their lives.

By the time I moved in, I think my housemates knew their time living there was running out. None of them were married; all were recently out of massage school, their practices young, their client lists short. In a few more months, their time together would break apart and scatter like seeds on the wind. Ironically, I would stay for a year or so after they'd left, albeit with a shifting set of housemates.

I knew I'd never stay long enough to plant flowers with the confidence that I would see them blossom the next summer, and the next. Yet some long-ago gardener, either tenant or owner, had done just that, planted seeds and seedlings. Perhaps this place was more than just a house to that gardener. It had once been someone's home, and home is where you want there to be beauty, want it enough to create it. Surely I wasn't the only one thankful for the daily beauty left behind by that long-gone stranger.

Now so many flowers waited for the bees. So many bees wanted nothing more than to wriggle their plump bodies into a flower's embrace and then dart to the next floral encounter. Their legs would be sticky with pollen that brought fertilization to the flowers and food to their hive's young. It was a relationship extending far back into prehistory, when bees (and other pollinators) and flowering plants developed their mutualistic relationship. Bees and other insects provide pollination, while plants reciprocate with nectar and other desired services. Bees are believed to have played a major role in the Cretaceous period's explosive rise of diverse flowering plant species. This long-standing relationship became so successful that now most of the world's flowering plants require insect (or other) pollination to reproduce.

Stepping carefully around the bees crawling across my rug, I glanced out the window at the hornets making their darting black flights. It's said that knowledge is power, but watching the ebony hornets gleaming in the sunlight, I wondered if knowledge wasn't power as much as it was intimacy. The more I had learned about the bees, the closer I had come to sharing their lives. No longer just some kind of a bug, the bees had become as real as my housemates, and with as much right to go about their lives.

But if I began to know anything about the hornets shielded behind the fragile grey walls of their nest, I wouldn't be able to call in the exterminators. I'd have to surrender the garage, and then the driveway and the backyard, and sooner or later my private basement entrance. I decided not to learn anything about hornets.

"Look!" my housemate Scott called out from the backyard. His tall, thin body loomed over our compost bin as he cried out, "Wasps! Wasps!"

Great, I thought as I walked back outside. *Bees in the bedroom. Hornets in the garage. Wasps in the compost bin. What's next? Hordes of locusts? Plagues of grasshoppers?*

Scott pointed to a compost bin beneath a western redcedar's sheltering limbs. I frowned as I noticed neat rows of diamond-shaped holes lining the bin's emerald-green plastic walls. If I were a queen bee looking for a nest, those holes would look like an opening to a grass-lined cavity. And this was exactly what the compost bin had become. No one in the house knew how to compost. For years, lawn clippings and weeds had been thrown in the bin and forgotten.

There were no wasps in sight, but soon enough a bumble bee alighted on an opening, quickly disappearing inside the bin. Another bee emerged from the same hole and took off for the daisies, followed by another bee. Hovering in the air was a bee eager to get into the bin.

Forager traffic, I thought with quiet satisfaction. The bees were returning to the nest, their legs thick with pollen, while others were flying out to find food for the colony. Despite the exterminators' assessment, the bees were nesting *outside*. Despite what seemed like common sense to humans, the bees were slipping through the cracks in my window frame and from there into my bedroom and office. So every time I turned on my full-spectrum office lights, the bees would circle my shoulders as I wrote grants for food banks and domestic violence shelters.

I explained to my housemates that the "wasps" were actually bees, and lived outside the house, not inside, but these distinctions mattered little. House meetings and impromptu kitchen gatherings only led to talk of sprays and traps. How could I argue? The house's basement was so large that in addition to my two rooms it also included a cavernous family room, created by some long-removed owner, where my housemates gave their clients massages. And what nearly naked person slathered in floral-scented massage oil could relax with bees buzzing about?

The house wasn't just a place of business for my housemates, though. It was their home, where they shared meals and friendships, arguments and intimacy. But where was mine?

By now, I'd been living in Seattle for over a decade, and I was still making no promises as to how long I'd stay. For a long time, home was like this current one, simply my most recent place, its walls adorned with turquoise and mauve scarves, and pictures of peregrine falcons and red-tailed hawks. Atop its bookcases were jars of loose change, seashells, and sticks of lemongrass incense. When my life shifted—a new job, a sudden illness, a new lover—I would move on to the next place, leaving another old place behind. But wasn't a real home that sweet, thorny place of commitments and comradeship where you lose the freedom to just wander off anywhere anytime? I wasn't sure I wanted a real home if that meant losing my freedom to leave.

But my freedom was lost even if I was slow to understand that. The temporary homes were the rentals filled with an ever-changing array of roommates over the years. My roots needed to go somewhere, and so my permanent home became that larger, if ever-changing, landscape. With every afternoon at a stream surveying salmon, with every field trip to learn about birds and botany, mosses and lichens, with every salvage or tree-planting, my hands got dirtier, and more of this place got under my skin. For all I talked (sometimes) about moving to Portland or San Francisco to once again find a better life in a different place, the words I didn't say were that I was finding it hard to imagine living somewhere else.

Which was just as well, because while I didn't know it at the time, my life was shifting once again. A month or so after moving into the house, I'd gone to a swing dance, where I'd met an English major turned scientist, then employed as a University of Washington data analyst and medical researcher. Jim Scanlan was newly arrived in Seattle, having grown up in the Northeast and later going to college and then graduate school in the Great Lakes region. I ran into him again at zydeco and contra dances, and of course at the Northwest Folklife Festival, Seattle's four-day celebration of all things music and dance. When we weren't dancing, we talked of science and books.

Our marriage would be years away. Our daughter was too far into our future to even imagine. Yet it was a future I was walking toward even if all I did those days was dodge the bees buzzing about incessantly. As beleaguered as I felt, I still couldn't call in the exterminators with their deadly chrysanthemum sprays and eco-green jumpsuits.

A WEEK AFTER THE DISCOVERY of the bees in the compost bin, I was complaining about them to one of my regular dance partners at a contra dance. During the waltz break, he introduced me to a local beekeeper.

"Removing the bees won't be a problem," she said, with an easy smile and a shining confidence at the first mention of the word *bees*. "I'll get the nest and set them up in my garden. It's filled with flowers. They'll do fine."

"These aren't honey bees," I warned. "They're bumble bees. They're worthless to you."

She waved her hand nonchalantly, and I glanced down at the yellow business card she had given me. Embossed in black ink was an illustration of an ebony-haired woman wearing a long Victorian gown not so very different from her own floral-print dress. The woman on the card gazed in seeming contentment at a hive encircled by bees. *Beauty and the Bees Honey* read the card. *Sally Harris, Beekeeper.*

Bees are bees to this woman, I thought, *and she's one of them.*

"How much will it cost?"

"Nothing. But I'll need help," cautioned Sally as she sipped her ice water. She tugged her hand through her thick black curls. "Someone will have to suit up to help capture them."

"Really?" I asked. What was it that Lord Peter Wimsey said in the mystery novel *Gaudy Night* about how we're supposed to suffer for our principles, and if we didn't, those principles weren't doing their job? My principles as a restoration volunteer and lay naturalist had kept me from calling in the exterminators. But what good were those principles if I abandoned the bees now? And what had been the point of all those hours and months and years of planting trees and lobbying senators, ripping out weeds and raising money, and any of the other ways I tried to repair the world if I couldn't do the small, right thing of relocating the bees where I lived? Trapped in the sticky web of my good intentions, I smiled weakly and said, "I can do that."

Sally came by late the next afternoon with an empty gallon yogurt container, trowels, hand hoes, and two white beekeeper suits. I picked up the thin suit with dismay.

"I thought these were made out of canvas."

"Oh, no," Sally said with a smile as she slipped off her sandals. "Just cotton. That's usually thick enough."

"What do we wear under it?" I asked.

Sally shrugged. "This is fine," she said, indicating our pastel tank tops and shorts. "But you'll need boots to stuff the pants into."

I ran into my bedroom and pulled my hiking boots from my closet. I also pulled out my long-sleeved polypro shirt, making sure to zip up the neck after I yanked it on over my tank top. I tugged the matching polypro pants on over my hiking shorts.

Sally stared when I returned. I said only, "If the bees don't get me, the heat will."

I stepped into the one-piece bee suit, flipped the black mesh hood over my head, and secured it with an intricate array of zippers and Velcro. Impervious to the bees (or so I hoped), we advanced on the compost bin and tipped it over. A buzzing black cloud of bees flew up, so many darting and circling that I couldn't count them. Sally pulled a three-pronged hand hoe through the brambles and brown leaves. She scooped bees and egg clusters into the gallon yogurt container, closing it as she said, "I'm not seeing a queen."

My heart sank. The bumble bee workers' collective lives were dedicated to defending and feeding the colony. If the queen was still in the compost bin, it would only be a matter of time before the bees returned to my bedroom.

"Sally, we've got to find the queen," I insisted. Sally calmly pulled back clumps of scratchy twigs and moldy brown leaves. The buzzing grew to a dull roar. Bees swooped. Bees encircled my head. Bees darted between my arms and legs. Like honey bees, bumble bees sting mainly to defend their nest. Unlike honey bees, bumble bees don't die when they sting. I could be stung over and over, enclosed by a thick ebony cloud of enraged bees.

One bee droned louder than the others. Primal instinct rooted me in place. I swirled my eyes sideways. A bumble bee was perched on my hood not two inches from my left eye.

"I need to get away from the bees," I croaked.

Sally nodded, unperturbed as she kept searching for the queen. I stepped from the cedar tree's shadows and back into the afternoon sunlight. It was only three feet—but that was far enough for the bees. I was out of the orbit of their tattered hive and lost queen. I was beyond the range of their interest.

I stood breathing hard, sweat clinging to my clothes, as drawn to the sunlight as the bees were. Our worlds were so different. What the bees sensed was so alien to what I saw and knew. The light we could share: that same distant warmth keeping us alive.

I let myself feel my terror as I stood still in the sunlight's brilliance. I stayed put until I could breathe normally. Then I walked back to Sally, who was unconcerned by the whirling bees.

Sally handed me the scratched yogurt container.

"I've looked everywhere," she said, "and still can't find any queens."

"Queens?" I stammered out. I stared at Sally in confusion and frustration. Successions in honey bee hives are fights to the death.

Invading or resident bumble bee queens can be killed in competitions over nest sites. "Queens? There's only one to a nest."

"That's honey bees."

"I don't want to hear this," I moaned. What I would later learn was that bumble bee nests sometimes have an old queen and several young queens that haven't left to find their wintering sites.

"Look, there may be several queens in this nest, or there may be just one. Either way, I haven't found a queen. She may be flying. We'll never catch her then."

"I thought queens only flew on their mating flights or when they swarmed," I said, frowning. I knew that mating flights were a queen honey bee's initiation from virginity to lifelong motherhood. Another way bumble bees differed from honey bees, I would later learn, was that queen bumble bees retain the ability to fly and forage as needed.

"Want me to check the container in case I got a queen without realizing it?"

We put the yogurt container on the rickety picnic table. Carefully, Sally opened the lid.

"There she is!" Sally cried. She slammed the lid shut, giving me only a brief glimpse of a bee larger and more elongated than the plump fuzzy workers.

Sally left with the queen and what we hoped were enough workers to start the hive anew. I could see a dozen or more bees circling the destroyed hive or dropping down to explore the moist brown darkness that had sheltered their queen. Within a few hours, most had disappeared into the sunlight and the sweet embrace of irises and snapdragons. Some would die soon, their legs sticky with pollen they no longer needed.

The hornets were soon gone, too. The next day, I came back from grocery shopping just as the exterminator was pulling out of our driveway. In this case, ignorance was power. A single hornet circled where the nest used to be. Scraps of papery grey walls skittered in the late afternoon breeze. No sense of obligation could make me miss them.

I called Sally. She had placed the bees ("along with some leaf mulch so they'll feel at home") under the rhododendron bushes in her front yard. Now bumble bees were buzzing and nuzzling flowers wherever she looked.

I walked out to the compost bin. There was no buzzing in my ears. Nothing small and black darted past me or glinted in the sunset glow. Relief mingled with sadness. Somewhere the bees from my garden were sinking into a gladiola or pink dahlia before daylight ebbed away. Now that I was no longer living with the bees I could appreciate their simple, unfailing perseverance.

Life is short. And full of flowers.

{ squire creek }

It was once again Yom Kippur, and I was north of Seattle, at Squire Creek. Sunlight dazzled between rainstorms. Around me, uprooted, wind-worn trees lay scattered like I Ching sticks. Squire Creek forked, with one thin spur dead-ending in rock and shifting sandbars.

As a child, all I knew of Yom Kippur were the long temple services, the stiff clothes, and the ritual fast that prohibited food or water. I never asked my father, the most observant one in our family, what he experienced on what is considered the holiest day of the year. My father, dead some fifteen years, was a fading memory, and my prayers were halting. I slipped my hand into Squire Creek's cold water and wondered if what I had read was true, that Yom Kippur's sundown-to-sundown fast and seemingly interminable services were intended to lead not to guilt but to joy and a repaired harmony in our relationship not just with family and community, but with God.

I sat near a pool where the water was still and dark. In it, dying pink salmon circled beneath a slow, swirling mosaic of gold conifer needles, amber cedar fronds, and bits of ebony-edged bone lichen. I found a pink salmon stranded at the pool's edge. He had the look of a pugilist battling unfavorable odds—a dark squat body, fanged distended jaws. Fungus, as gold as an ancient coin, tinged the pink's humped back. His jaws pumped open-shut-open-shut, pushing sand and iridescent water over his gills.

It had been two years since I last saw pink salmon. In the coastal streams of Asia and North America that still have salmon, one run of pinks will spawn in each even-numbered year, while a second, genetically distinct run spawns in odd-numbered years. Washington State's pinks spawn almost exclusively in odd-numbered years. In that visit two years before, Squire Creek had shimmered in its flow past western redcedar trees. RVs had rumbled into the creekside campground. I'd heard the steady pounding of State Route 530's traffic echoing past horse pastures and roadside espresso huts.

I'd stood shivering in that distant fall day's thin rain, realizing that what I had at first thought were stones and twists of current were instead pink salmon holding still, facing upstream and resisting the fast downstream flow of water. Their white underbellies blended with the mottled stones beneath them. Three, four, a dozen were nearly hidden in the dull, shifting light reflecting off the creek. The males' humps protruded above the water, then sank beneath the flow and rose up again, an elusive clue to their presence.

The pink salmon twitching at my feet this year was probably conceived during that distant fall run. I leaned back against an uprooted tree and watched him. Gold and silver motes swirled in the morning light above the dying fish. He lay flat against the stones and clear water at the pool's edge. His speckled olive-grey tail jerked up. He was still again.

Brief weeks before, the pink was sleek and silvery as he traversed the North Pacific and Puget Sound. Following the age-old cycle, the pink left the estuary and swam upstream. His muscles softened. His body darkened, and his skin thickened. Hooked jaws and the male's characteristic hump formed. His gonads matured for mating, his digestive organs atrophied, and he stopped feeding. He began living off his own body's stored fat.

This pink was at the end of a short, two-year life, and weakening. The creek's fast current must have pushed him from the deep water into the pool where the creek had cut into its bank. Pale rain-soft bodies of dead pink and Chinook salmon were tangled in the dirt-flecked roots of alder, cedar, and fir. Yet this still-living lone pink is one of the lucky ones. Pinks are the most abundant of Pacific salmon, but upward of an estimated 95 percent fall prey to fishing fleets and the waiting jaws of a vast ocean.

The pink's tail heaved. *Smack.* The fish was still. Another heave. *Smack. Smack.* His soft belly was now firm against the gravel. His dark fungus-mottled body towered above the clear water. He jerked his tail back and forth, back and forth. He swam forward, toward me and away from the pool's center. He swam to where the trickle of creek ended in gritty sand and broken twigs. He fell back on his side. He was still, except for the slow pumping of his jaws.

I WAS RAISED TO BE afraid of death, the end of life, the void—my father's stroke, the pneumonia the doctors said would kill him. Only my father didn't die then, just as he didn't die after another round of pneumonia, and eventually the doctors said they no longer knew when he would die, that they could only promise my father's life would continue on for days, weeks, months, possibly years in a white-walled hospital room filled with dripping IVs, whispers, silence.

This pink's impending death is not the death I was taught to fear. It is not death at all if death means finality, cessation, rupture. In their death, salmon are the great gift of life.

The Pacific salmon's return, death, and eventual decay bring nitrogen, phosphorous, carbon, and other nutrients to the forests surrounding salmon rivers and streams. The pink salmon will return to Squire Creek's remaining forests, and in death, the eye sockets of those salmon will be picked clean by hungry forest creatures, their twisted skeletons cloaked by fallen alder leaves, as if ready to swim out of the moist earth and back to the river. If I came back in a day or a week, I would find fins, grey flesh, and bone between the tight curls of sword-fern fronds, the mossy rocks, and the gnarled umber roots, as if the distant ocean had come to land and reinvigorated a forest. Which it has.

Salmon gain well over 90 percent of their weight feeding in the ocean. When they return to the Pacific Northwest's nutrient-poor forests and streams, they bring in their flesh and bones the marine-derived nutrients that serve as a natural fertilizer, spurring the growth of Sitka spruce and other native trees. The faster the trees grow, the sooner that growth can create the kinds of stream-side habitat salmon need, where shade cools the water, and where falling limbs and branches break and vary the stream flow, forming the sheltered pools and hiding places young salmon need to evade predators. Fallen twigs, branches, and other organic debris can also snag a salmon carcass, preventing it from being washed downstream, and keeping it where it can benefit a stream's flora and fauna.

"The great essence will flower in our lives and expand throughout the world. May we learn to let it shine so we can augment its glory" reads a modern variation of the Kaddish, the Jewish prayer for the dead. "We praise, we continue to praise, and yet whatever it is we praise is quite beyond the grasp of all these words . . . We know, yet we do not know."

One life dies; life itself never dies. This is the exchange of flesh and fin, the bits of bone now scattered between stones—through it all, the body decomposes to carbon, nitrogen, and other essential nutrients for life in the watershed. Life has been on Earth some 3.5 to 4 billion years. More than 1.3 million species have been named and recorded. Thousands more are discovered yearly. How many millions more species share our world is anyone's guess, and some recent estimates have gone as high as 8.7 million and upward. But among the known creatures are the species of the genus *Oncorhynchus*— Pacific salmon—which, while the species themselves have existed for millions of years, recolonized and claimed permanent residence in the Pacific Northwest only about ten thousand years ago.

IN THE KABBALAH, the Jewish mystical tradition, God's essence is believed to once have been contained in holy vessels that broke upon arriving in this earthly realm, scattering and hiding sparks of divine, generative light amid flesh, bone, and stone. "Every day the glory is ready to emerge from its debasement," wrote Rabbi Nachman in the eighteenth century.

My father's joys were brief and his illnesses long, but he was a devout man. For decades I was angry that God didn't intervene and prevent his suffering; I was angrier that I didn't either. Looking back, I understand now that I needed to leave my old home in New York after my father's death and journey out, not so much to break with the past as to see it anew. I needed a new and unknown place where I could stumble, explore, and begin to grasp that if death is our realm's old, worn coin, then waiting to emerge from its hum-bling, perhaps debasing, exchange is life.

A desiccated white moth twisted in the broken strands of a spider's web. The pink at the edge of the creek's pool moved his gills in slow, slight pumping; his tail slapped faintly. My breath. My father's breath. "You have nothing to do but live," wrote the late Pacific Northwest poet Jody Aliesan. And my father did live. He died when he was the happiest he had been in years, having discovered a local senior center. There his friendliness, courtesy, and curiosity shone. The staff loved him. Others did too, I'm sure. He had nothing to do but live, because life is inevitable, inexhaustible, and death is simply life in another form.

After all these years of September, October, November, and December watching pink, Chinook, coho, sockeye, and chum salmon fully alive as they die, I am no longer so afraid to be near death. I was terrified years ago in my father's narrow hospital room. Our decision to end life support embarked my father on a journey through days and nights of whispered begging for ice chips to ease starvation. The guilt is still there. The guilt will always be there. But it has a balance now. A spark of joy has been kindled. My father's bones became ashes that became the earth between the roots of an orange tree, became stone, feather, fin, the dark fleck of an eye.

WIND POURED THROUGH moss-draped alder. Cedar boughs swayed in its wake. Creaks turned to a snap; a thin branch of lichen-dappled alder fell on the sandbar. I used it to gently push the pink into deeper water. Death would come soon enough to him, I knew, either as spawning's inevitable shadow or perhaps the tearing paws of a raccoon. The pink slipped through the murky water. He snapped weakly before taking his place beside another male.

To mate and die in the place you were born; this is the only perfect circle I know in an imperfect world.

{ the duwamish river }

A Sara's orange-tip butterfly fluttered above the tangled mounds of Himalayan blackberry. In a nearby stand of trees, I crawled belly-down across wood bark, brittle brown leaves, and purple plums shriveling where the August sun had slipped between tree limbs. I looked for the thorny spines of Himalayan blackberry to snip. Weeding is like plugging your finger in the dike between native species and invasive ones. Pull it out, and in rushes exuberant life to take root in a new home.

This morning's weeding expedition, organized by a local restoration group, had brought a half dozen people to volunteer at T-107 (more formally known as Terminal 107 Park), a "pocket park" in Seattle, nestled between the Duwamish River and the vehicle traffic on West Marginal Way Southwest. When I could navigate the tangle of highways to get there outside of spawning season, T-107 was perhaps ten minutes by car from Longfellow Creek, where I'd spent the last several falls monitoring returning coho and chum.

Longfellow flows into the Duwamish, which was among the places the Duwamish Tribe called home, and later, generations of European immigrants. Now the Duwamish hosts barges, factories,

Port of Seattle docks, and small parks of reclaimed habitat. T-107's reclamation was a small part of the sustained effort to restore as much as was still possible of the Duwamish, once an important local river for spawning salmon and now a Superfund cleanup site.

Himalayan blackberry is an invasive weed as abundant in the Pacific Northwest as the rain. I'll admit the anthropomorphism and say it's as nonnative to Puget Sound as I am. Perhaps no other restoration volunteering makes me remember so strongly that I'm an ex–New Yorker transplanted to Seattle, and that one weed is ripping out another to make a home for native species.

I used to love yanking Himalayan blackberry from the earth, tearing away the deep-rootedness common to unwanted creatures. With every righteous uprooting, I felt more firmly in place, as if I was closing ranks with the locals to protect my newfound home from invaders. I especially craved that unthinking satisfaction once the era of changing addresses and housemates was over for me. The Montlake house's massage therapists had long since moved to new cities and houses, replaced by too many other housemates to remember, until I'd made the jump to my own apartment, where the higher rent had been an incentive that spurred on my business.

For the last few years, sunlight had shone on my desk, and solitude had alternated with book clubs and parties. While I was more rooted in one place since I'd moved to Seattle, paradoxically my enthusiasm for all this tearing out and pulling up was waning. In fact, I was questioning whether it made sense at all. Is the Himalayan blackberry really an ecological criminal to be ripped out willy-nilly? Or is it part of our home regardless of our diligent weeding?

At T-107, wooden fences were entwined with a verdant wall of Himalayan blackberry. Not far below flowed the Duwamish River with its white-and-blue tugboats and its wood pylons, where bald eagles and great blue herons perched. T-107 used to be the site of a brick factory. Now foot trails meandered amid alder and hip-high seedlings of western redcedar, Douglas fir, and other conifers. Nestled under these young trees were Himalayan blackberry stems thin as pencils and low to the ground. I identified the weed by its thorns and three to five-leaf sets and snipped it with my hand shears where it emerged from the shadowed ground.

I had uprooted the blackberry at restoration sites along the Snoqualmie River, Bellevue's Mercer Slough, and many other Seattle and King County habitats, often as part of salmon recovery efforts. Unlike T-107, which has been weeded many times, at those other sites, the Himalayan blackberry was taller than I am. I would wear workingmen's leather gloves so stiff I could hardly grasp the pruning shears. I would sever a cane only to have a botanical chaos of vines and thorns jerk up like a tightly stretched tent snapping a pole. Canes longer than my arms, my legs, my body would clutch me. Thick maroon thorns would cut through muddy jeans and flannel shirts to rip crimson streaks into my skin.

Even so, as I was doing at T-107, I cut as close to the ground as I could get. The Himalayan blackberry would grow back. I would return to cut it. The Himalayan blackberry would grow back. I would return and cut again. The Himalayan blackberry would grow back weaker, but still alive, still growing. I would return and cut and admire the weed's persistence, its tenacity to take root, its fierceness to live.

I'm ambivalent about weeds. I am one.

ALTHOUGH I IDENTIFY with weeds, it's not always clear to me just what a weed *is*. Definitions vary, often contradicting, and can get as tangled as what grows in an abandoned lot. From an agricultural perspective, a weed is a plant that causes economic harm. From an ecological perspective, a weed is a plant that thrives where humans have disturbed the landscape. Reading the definition in my *Webster's Third New International Dictionary*, I found listed amid some six column inches of text "an obnoxious growth, thing, or person"; "one of wild or rank growth"; "an article or style of dress usually black worn as a sign of mourning," and my favorites, "a sudden illness or relapse" and an "attack of madness." Not surprisingly, the verb forms cluster around variations of removing or being freed from something undesirable. Adding to the botanic and semantic chaos is that one person's weed is another person's pretty flower.

The easiest way through the definition thicket is to say weeds are plants that show up in a place where we don't want them and that won't go away. Poison or pull them all you want, weeds come back, asserting their grip over the landscape. If anything, all our picking, poisoning, and other eradication efforts can act as a form of natural selection, promoting hardier, more genetically diverse weeds that are better able to thrive alongside us.

For most people, *weed* doesn't take into account whether a plant is native to an area or a nonnative species. But it's a distinction that matters to anyone engaged in environmental restoration. Native plants are typically species that came to a region by wind, wave, or some other natural means that didn't involve humans. Once in a place, natives reproduce and thrive without human involvement. This is different from what happens with nonnative species, whereby humans intentionally or accidentally take plants or other species out of their natural region and bring them into a new place.

The United States is a nation of immigrants, and as with people, so with plants. Potatoes came from South America. Apples and pears were introduced from Eurasia. We can thank Luther

Burbank, the famed botanist, for bringing the Himalayan black-berry to the United States in 1885. But it doesn't matter whether these newcomers came because we wanted them or they arrived as stowaways in our cargo. These and many other plants have become part of the world we know as home. Most nonnative or introduced species (estimates are as high as 90 percent) behave much like their human immigrant counterparts. They find an unfilled niche, settle in alongside the natives, and add to the local biodiversity without harming it, which, speaking as a weed, is what I hope I'm doing.

Invasives are a special group of nonnatives—namely, those that harm human health, the environment, or the economy. Invasives are also a leading driver of native plant extinction. Himalayan blackberry has all the classic characteristics of an invasive. It repro-duces quickly (8,300 to 15,500 seeds per square yard, dispersed by foraging birds and mammals, or by "daughter" canes that can grow twenty-three feet in a season). It thrives in human-induced dis-ruption. Tear down a forest for suburban roads, shopping malls, or megachurches, and Himalayan blackberry moves in, taking root in gated communities as easily as alongside rivers, streams, wetlands, or forests.

It's been a century or so since Seattle underwent waves of log-ging, but while maple, alder, and other deciduous trees grew back, native conifers like western redcedar and Douglas fir, which should have returned through natural botanical succession, never really took root. This is, in part, because of competition from invasive species like the Himalayan blackberry.

In 2005, a local newspaper reported that the Himalayan black-berry on Seattle's public lands could cover more than nine hundred football fields—and that wasn't counting what was in backyards. More recently, Seattle's Urban Forest Stewardship Plan predicted that within one hundred years the city's forested lands would be "dominated" by invasives, with most trees and native vegetation gone, unless Himalayan blackberry and its ilk were controlled. After clearing even a small thicket at restoration projects, I've found fertile soil barren of salmonberry, thimbleberry, Oregon grape, and many other native plants that once thrived here. I have found stunted, pencil-thin seedlings of cedar, fir, and other native trees swarmed by blackberry, its vines climbing over and choking the native plants as it grabs the sunlight, rain, nutrients. The native plants die out. The Himalayan blackberry survives. For a weed to be considered invasive, it has to go beyond being unwanted. It must take over the landscape and block out other species. Not all introduced species do this, and neither do all weeds. Himalayan blackberry does.

David Quammen's elegiac essay "Planet of Weeds" describes how, in the biological sense, *weeds* can refer not just to plants but also to mammals, birds, fish, or other species with the common characteristics that "they reproduce quickly, disperse widely when given a chance, tolerate a fairly broad range of habitat conditions, take hold in strange places, succeed especially in disturbed eco-systems, and resist eradication once they're established. They are scrappers, generalists, opportunists."

Think of rats. Think of starlings. Think of us. Humans aren't simply the most destructive invasive species on the planet. We are, as Quammen says, "the consummate weed."

At T-107, the tangled relationship between weeds and home was on my mind as I ripped a hank of Himalayan blackberry off a stack of cut wood. What was revealed were black bugs, dirt, and stones juxtaposed with brand-new shadows cast by the summer sunlight. A brown-and-grey moth fluttered down to the newly exposed habitat. I blinked my eyes, and it appeared to be just another leaf amid the scattered brown leaves.

For most of my years in Seattle, I didn't think weeding at T-107 (or any other site) required careful thought. Weeding seemed full of uncontestable good intentions: take out the Himalayan black-berry and other invasives; plant Nootka rose or other native species; provide needed habitat—a home—for resident or migratory birds and other wildlife, or re-create riparian habitat for young salmon in their freshwater phase; restore T-107 to approximate (within the limits of what is possible) what it was like when the Duwamish was a healthy wild river bursting with salmon.

Washington State estimates that Seattle and King County's population will grow from 2.1 million people in 2015 to 2.4 million people by 2040. Many of these people will be immigrants like me who come to enjoy Puget Sound's once-pristine beaches, Cascade and Olympic mountain trails, and nearby national parks. Our arrival only increases the economic incentives to turn habitat into urban or suburban developments, which helps push already overexploited salmon and other local beleaguered species closer to extinction. The longer I live in Seattle, the less my restoration volunteering has become about learning about the place, and the more it has become about minimizing my impact.

For years, good intentions (along with leather gloves and hand shears) were all I needed to yank Himalayan blackberry anywhere I chanced upon it. But even good intentions require scrutiny. Was I only ripping out an invasive weed? Or was I helping plant something else just as noxious?

Writers such as Michael Pollan and Stephen Jay Gould have rightly noted how the ecological issues surrounding native and nonnative species can become co-opted by "antinative" political or social agendas, with the nadir being Nazi Germany's efforts to "cleanse" so-called "unwholesome alien influences" even in the form of plants, such as *Impatiens parviflora*, a small woodland flower.

Knowing this gives me pause when, closer to home, I encounter a zeal extending to outright hatred of weeds, invasives, or just plain nonnative species.

The ecological jargon surrounding nonnatives *is* xenophobic: filled with aliens, exotics, nonindigenous, foreign, or introduced species that make it sound as if crazed hordes are storming the city gates. "The invaders must be stopped!" screamed one memorable email about a weeding. "Know Your Enemy" shrieked a headline on an otherwise informative website about invasive species. A page on a joint university and local government website about "The Ten Most Un-Wanted Pests" had a fact sheet designed like a law enforcement "wanted" poster, complete with Himalayan blackberry's crimes ("trespassing on private property, overrunning desired plants"), "accomplices" to the "perpetrators" (birds that eat the berries and pass seeds through their digestive systems, taking blackberry to new locations), and steps for dealing with this "intense criminal" ("send in the S.W.A.T. team," a.k.a. weeders like me) since "there's no killing this monster." An invasive-species field guide, edited by respected biologists, says of Himalayan blackberry and the also invasive evergreen blackberry, "The delicious fruit creates . . . the reluctance to treat these two species as vicious invaders."

I've seen the converse, too, with native species described as more natural, better fitted to a place—and having a right to it. They are described as fragile and displaced, made refugees in their own home due to a motley mob of weeds, aliens, and invasives. John Tallmadge, in his book *The Cincinnati Arch*, writes of an assumed "cherished concept of Edenic wilderness," a purity of nature that existed before we blundered onto the scene that underlies "every other value ascribed to native species and ecosystems."

Speaking again as a weed, I'd have to say that tenacity counts. Maybe the Himalayan blackberry has earned its place, if only because it's so hard to get rid of it. More than a few restoration volunteers I've spoken to voice my concern: Why penalize the plant for being hardy and able to tolerate new environments?

Native species, in contrast, tend to be wedded to a place, coevolved with other native species, and vulnerable to sustained human-driven environmental assaults—like paving wetlands to put in parking lots. While native plants are critical to a functioning ecosystem, I tend to agree with Stephen Jay Gould that natives are "only those organisms that first happened to gain and keep a footing." They are not always the species best suited to a place through all times or conditions, nor are they always superior to newcomer species.

Once in place, newcomers and natives interact and influence each other, each change leading to another. Even if it were possible to remove all nonnatives from a landscape, the result would not necessarily be the return of a preinvasion ecosystem.

Human travel is the main way that plants and animals leave an old place for a new one, whether seeds stuck to sandals, rats lurking in trade ships, or snakes coiled in food shipments. Every forest cut down for suburban housing, every shoreline developed for economic reasons, destroys habitat for natives—and opens the landscape to weeds and invasives. Research on climate change is showing that weeds thrive in the hotter carbon dioxide-enriched environments that are becoming our planet's future. Combine climate change with habitat destruction and a fast global-transport system, and Quammen's weed-overrun planet looms.

Maybe blaming the weeds is just human nature. Building the political clout and economic punch needed to preserve land for wildlife, or plan urban and suburban areas for sustainability, is hard. Changing personal behavior enough to keep indoors that beloved invasive species, the pet cat, an all-too-local predator that's destroying bird populations, is even harder. Yanking a plant we don't like is easy.

After two hours spent weeding at T-107, though, the hypocrisy was stinging me, along with the thorn scratches on my arms. I couldn't ignore any longer how inequitable (if not ridiculous) it is that we human weeds go hither and yon, bringing other weeds, aliens, and invasives with us, then vilifying the newcomers we've brought and ripping them out in the name of restoring habitat for the natives. But I had a personal issue to wrestle with as I snipped thorny spines of Himalayan blackberry, smelling the fragrance of verdant life with each cut. I'm ambivalent about weeds because it took a weed to help me make a home.

I could yank out the unwanted flora all I wanted, and while it would help me feel less like a weed and more like a native closing the door on unwanted outsiders, it didn't change the fact that I was an outsider myself. No matter how many years I'd lived in Seattle, I still heard that I was "so New York" in my speech, attitudes, and expectations. (Okay, okay. The *New York Times* was my browser's homepage for far too many years, I think strong opinions make for a fun evening, and while I've learned what a latte is, coffee isn't my favorite drink and certainly not my regular one.) The subtext wasn't subtle: I (still) didn't belong; I (still) had things to learn when I looked around. The latter is one of the advantages of being a weed, and I wouldn't want to change that even if I could. Learning about a home, as I had to, requires really looking at a place (something that a region's longtimers may forget to do) and, rather like the weeds I was pulling out at restoration events, digging in and remaining where you didn't originally belong.

Like many people, whether native or newcomer, I'm "plant-blind." I don't bother to see plants other than as a blur of wind-shifting green leaves unless I make an effort to notice them.

Volunteering at invasive-species removals forced me to explore what was growing in my new home. At T-107, I learned to recognize another local weed, the common tansy, a plant with long stalks ending in feather-like fronds and a crown of yellow-gold button flowers. It was only then that I realized that I had been seeing (and ignoring) common tansy in my backyard all summer long. After years of restoration volunteering, I can never remember the field marks for Pacific silver fir, a native tree species. But, even in winter, without its purple-black berries to pop in my mouth, I can identify the Himalayan blackberry. It's a botanical landmark that reminds me of where I am: in this park, weeding along this river, living in this city.

Before finishing the morning's weeding at T-107, I yanked and snipped at a round hill of two invasives: morning glory and bull thistle. What was revealed was a thicket of snowberry and red-osier dogwood, two native plants. Curling at the thicket's edges, waiting its chance, was Himalayan blackberry. Regardless of my respect for it, the more abundant the Himalayan blackberry, the fewer other plants there are alongside it. As plant variety shrinks, so does local biodiversity, with a smaller number and a less diverse range of birds and small mammals able to find the food, water, shelter, and other ecological services they need. My world has become immeasurably larger by learning about the small creatures living in it. The less there is for me to explore, the smaller my home will become.

By midday I, with five other volunteers, gathered alongside our thirty-gallon garbage bags filled with morning glory, thistle, and blackberry. There was no one here I would likely see again, and if I did, I might not recognize them anyway. Yet I was reassured that they would be in this city, people who in large ways or small ones help repair the world that is close at hand.

We said our good-byes as a train rumbled past. A belted king-fisher rattled a call. I smelled the briny tang of the Duwamish, watched cargo boats ply toward the Port of Seattle, and reached a bittersweet epiphany: My life had included many homes of place and heart—jobs, bioregions, politics, writing. Soon Jim and I would be married, and that would become another kind of home, one where long-standing patterns would root and unexpected changes would blossom, one that would take me years to under-stand. I may be a weed, but I've lived in Seattle long enough to understand the natural world of its past and present, and to care about its future.

I've not traveled as far or rooted as well as the Himalayan black-berry, but I can say that home is not just a geographic place or the creatures in it. Home is your attitude toward the place you're in. Home is where you're rooted through exploration and engage-ment. That's what makes Seattle my home now. Maybe what I was restoring at T-107 wasn't native plants but the human obligation to be engaged with the place where we live.

I'll never get rid of the Himalayan blackberry. I'm not even sure I want to. Maybe the best I can do—maybe all I want—is to keep a balance between native and newcomer. Give the Himalayan blackberry sun, soil, wind, and birds to disperse its seeds, and it will outlast me. And through human choice and tenacity, and a lot of weeding, so will the native plants.

{ longfellow creek }

Late September

Every fall during my five years monitoring salmon at Longfellow Creek, I drove along the Alaskan Way Viaduct; the elevated highway passes Seattle's downtown towers and Elliott Bay's waterfront and ferry terminals, and leads onto the West Seattle Bridge. Below the bridge are the Port of Seattle's cargo terminals and cranes and the Duwamish River's West Waterway. The West Waterway, busy and industrial, opens into a culvert that makes it possible for spawning coho and chum salmon to leave the river and swim beneath city streets and a steel mill until the culvert "daylights" and the fish enter Longfellow Creek's downstream rush. From the Avalon Way exit (where a sign reads "Welcome to Luna Park"), I pass a glassblowing studio and then a café, and then go down Southwest Yancy Street to a fitness center, where I park. And as I do every September, I think, *This is a weird place for a salmon stream.*

On this day, Longfellow Creek was so low it seemed little more than light glimmering over stones. Five house sparrows took flight as I rested my data-collection form atop the footbridge's wooden railing and marked my session's start time. I put on polarized sunglasses. I watched the creek for a twist of movement, for a dorsal fin slipping through light-rippled water. I waited.

The drive to Longfellow had been along the same route as always, but my starting point was different this day. Gone was my cozy one-bedroom apartment, just a few blocks from Green Lake Park, my shelter as I grew my business and as my relationship with Jim deepened. That apartment was now yet another place of my past, and I'd found a new home just a few blocks from my old one. All those long-ago moves had given me a certain skill in uprooting my life and replanting it in a new place. Age-shredded socks and torn T-shirts aren't the only old, unnecessary parts of myself that I'd learned to leave behind. Or at least I was hoping so, because this time I was moving not just into a new house but a new life, as Jim and I had decided to move in together.

I brought my attention back to watching the creek. The fall rains hadn't yet started. Once they did, the rain would increase the river and stream flows pouring into Puget Sound estuaries, and signal to the salmon waiting that there's sufficient water to begin their upstream migration. Since it was impossible to know for sure when the salmon would arrive at Longfellow, though, I found that it was best to start early. I wasn't at Longfellow for just my own reasons, after all, but as a citizen scientist gathering observational data on the types of salmon arriving and what they were doing, which basically meant I was waiting for something to happen. Three times a week for fifteen minutes per visit (at least), I waited and watched, alert yet relaxed, striving to accept the sudden—and not discount the unexpected. An alder limb might crash into the creek. Black-capped chickadees could call in the red-osier dogwood. More pertinent to my role, a coho or another salmon could search out the shelter of a downed tree that breaks the current. When I saw a fish, I marked the date and time, whether it was an adult or juvenile, and if it was dead or alive.

Different streams have different species, but at Longfellow, I expected unids (unidentifiable fish), coho salmon, or chum salmon, but I was also keeping an eye open for the threatened Puget Sound Chinook, as well as various trout. I marked down whether an external tag was present or an adipose fin was missing (coho and Chinook from local hatcheries have this small fin behind the dorsal fin removed prior to release). I noted if I talked with local people during my visit, or if anything at the stream seemed odd or required attention. My marks would join those of hundreds of volunteers who watch streams in the Lake Washington watershed, nearby Vashon Island, Seattle, and the central Puget Sound area to sketch a picture showing policy makers, scientists, and the public whether fall spawning salmon are returning to creeks and reaching spawning areas.

In the first years I searched out Western Washington's salmon streams, I interpreted the salmon as icons of home; as symbols of fertility, death, and transformation; as messengers bringing me an epiphany. Then my awareness changed. Not suddenly, but slowly. As I came to understand where I was and how to live here, the salmon became less symbols of a place and more fellow creatures living alongside me in it. Now I wonder if it's more respectful to see a creature as it is rather than how I want it to be.

Maybe gathering observational data means putting aside the desire for personal inspiration and seeing a place on its own terms. Is that what it means to be engaged in citizen science?

Some would say that simply gathering data doesn't make me a citizen who's also a scientist. For that, I would have to analyze and then craft meaning from the marks made on data forms or, at least, ask and possibly answer a few questions of my own. A question is a route out of boredom and into wonder, if I'm lucky. None of my questions, however, are scientific: What can I hope to find here?

Why should Longfellow, given all that's been done to it, be beautiful or bountiful? What will I see if I let myself see it?

I checked my watch, marked zeros on my form, wrote down the time my session ended, and only then left my site to wander along the creek's foot trail as it meandered along a stretch of Longfellow.

Near the Salmon Bone Bridge, I found a *Russula* mushroom growing alongside a big-leaf maple. I'd seen turtles there in past, sunnier falls, mainly red-eared sliders that are most likely abandoned pets (or their offspring), like the ones I've seen at Green Lake Park. There were no turtles on this day. Instead, the Himalayan blackberry was thick with fruit, some berries black and drying out, others red and rushing toward ripeness against the coming winter. But what was drawing my attention was an office chair, upright in the creek, water flowing between its wheels. There was no trash can or computer station, so I suppose whoever left the chair wasn't setting up an office.

Salmon monitoring has its protocols, one of which is that volunteers aren't supposed to go into the stream. It's a bad example for the public, and theoretically I could crush a redd, although it was too early in the season to worry about that. *Tikkun olam*, on the other hand, has its own necessities. I hauled the chair onto the trail.

Early October

It was Yom Kippur, but I had eaten. Just as I was not fasting, I was also not praying. I had to assume that being at Longfellow as a citizen scientist went against the prohibition of working on Yom Kippur. All this added to an already impressive list of sins I was supposed to be considering on a day dedicated to atonement and reconciliation. Since I was tallying up all the things I was doing wrong, I should include that I was supposed to be counting fish at the Southwest Yancy footbridge and not clearing plant debris from the culvert. But if the culvert's grate is blocked with tangles of fallen tree limbs, leaves, and Himalayan blackberry vines, no salmon swimming up the Duwamish can enter Longfellow Creek. Seattle Public Utilities, which oversees all of the city's many creeks, clears the grate regularly, but leaves and twigs fall when they will and not according to government timetables.

So I shoved a branch into the water and used it to maneuver deadfall between the grate's bars. A channel opened, and with it, my pride in a job well done. Never mind that clearing the grate most likely led to biasing the data (although I *was* supposed to be out there watching for blockages and similar problems with the creek). All that mattered to me was that a fish streaked upstream. Another waited within the culvert, where it was too dark to identify the fish's field marks. Then a speckled fish with a scarred back and no adipose fin pushed forward, seemingly merging with the stream.

We had just had the first rainstorms in weeks, which meant Long-fellow held toxin-laden stormwater washed down from streets and roads. If these fish were coho (and they almost certainly were, since it was too early in the fall for chum), they'd probably be poisoned and dead all too soon. My pride might be another sin to ponder.

I pulled out my data form and scribbled *3 unids @ grate*. With luck, I would see them at the footbridge. With luck, they wouldn't be doing the *Jesus walk*, the term local newspapers had reported some people using to describe poisoned coho gyrating so wildly they appear to be walking on water. Longfellow typically receives more spawning coho than other Seattle streams or creeks (not counting the Duwamish River or the Ship Canal); some years have brought more than two hundred fish. Upward of 60 to 90 percent will fall victim to pre-spawn mortality, meaning they die before they have a chance to find a mate and lay eggs.

The life-history pattern where death closely follows reproduction, known as *semelparity*, is an evolutionary Faustian bargain that tends to occur in species with high juvenile survival but low adult survival, like salmon. During the transition from freshwater to salt water, and then while at sea, salmon face a host of natural predators and conditions that increase adult mortality, but which gives the survivors a chance to feed in rich ocean pastures, gain in size and strength, and build reserves for long, arduous journeys back to their natal creeks. Once at spawning grounds, generally speaking, larger females will outcompete smaller females in acquiring and guarding prime redd sites, and be more likely to lay large yolk-rich eggs that lead to larger size and better survival for young salmon.

Semelparity gives salmon no second chances to reproduce. Salmon can spawn and then die from an innately programmed death. Or, salmon can die before their once-in-a-lifetime chance to spawn. Death before spawning sometimes occurs in mature salmon returning to nonurban rivers and streams, but the process typically plays out over a period of weeks, with fish already weakened from a return migration and adjustment to freshwater succumbing due to low water flows that make it impossible to reach upstream spawning habitat, or from high water temperature, parasites, infections, or similar causes.

In Longfellow and other urban creeks across the Puget Sound region, however, pre-spawn mortality occurs soon after coho enter the stream. Newspapers have reported healthy adult coho losing their equilibrium, lurching to and fro, crashing about, and careening. I've seen something different but just as common. Fish lethargic in the water. Seemingly stunned. Fins splayed out. Mouths gaping open. Death is inevitable—not gentle, not quiet, but seemingly painful.

"One of the penalties of an ecological education is that one lives alone in a world of wounds," wrote Aldo Leopold, the late scientist and author of *A Sand County Almanac*, among other writing instrumental in developing contemporary thinking on conservation and environmental ethics. A loss of innocence, ecological or otherwise, is the proverbial birth of knowledge. The toxic stormwater pouring into Longfellow came from my actions and the actions of millions of other people living in this watershed and across the greater Seattle region. Stormwater runoff—rainwater flowing off our roads and rooftops, over parking lots and paved streets—contains oil and grease from cars, bacteria from pet or wildlife waste or from failing septic systems, soaps, dirt, and just about anything else that winds up on the street. Seattle's drainage system pipes some stormwater into sewers for treatment, but the rest pours directly into Longfellow and other creeks that flow into local lakes or Puget Sound, where stormwater accounts for some 75 percent of the pollution poisoning Puget Sound.

It's said that on Rosh Hashanah one is judged and on Yom Kippur one's fate is sealed, and the only things that can alter that fate are righteousness (usually the obligation to give wisely), prayers, and change of conduct. I've never been one for prayer, and besides, in the Jewish tradition it's said that atonement on Yom Kippur occurs only for harms between self and God. Harms to other humans require apology and forgiveness, and often some action to correct the damage. Agnostic or not, and no matter what my thoughts about prayer, I wouldn't have been at Longfellow if I didn't believe that same obligation extends to human actions toward this creek and the rest of the natural world. As I understand it, I (we) have the power to harm, and that same power gives me (us) an obligation to try and repair. Leopold's "world of wounds" is alive with *tikkun*'s opportunities.

Saying that knowledge brings responsibility is easy. Figuring out what to do is hard. *Tikkun* makes no promises as to the end result. It's as imperfect as the people putting it into action. The consequences of a repair can ripple out in unintended ways. Sometimes a repair repairs. Sometimes—like clearing the grate, perhaps—a seeming repair causes more harm than good. Other times a repair has the unexpected result of revealing hidden problems.

Longfellow Creek used to flow into the mudflats, saltwater sloughs, and marshes of the Duwamish River and the Elliott Bay estuaries. But sometime before 1920, the mudflats at nearby Young's Cove were filled to make way for an expanded steel mill. A culvert was built to allow Longfellow Creek to reach the Duwamish River, and from there flow into Elliott Bay, in order to avert a public health hazard from raw sewage that had been entering the creek. In the 1990s, Seattle began restoring its streams, and since then, gravel has been imported to form spawning areas, fish passage barriers have been removed, and native trees have been planted along Longfellow's lower reaches to provide shade and cool this riparian zone. However, it seemed that no one gave enough thought to stormwater's impact on water quality in Longfellow and other urban creeks until the coho accepted our invitation to return.

I thought back to that day long ago at Kelsey Creek when I'd held fertilized coho eggs in my hands before placing them in incubation tubes. Pre-spawn mortality was revealed just a few years after that. In the late 1990s, Seattle Public Utilities and Washington Trout (now the Wild Fish Conservancy) conducted field studies to see if habitat restoration was making it possible for adult salmon to reach and spawn in urban streams. Up and down creeks were seemingly healthy coho females bulging with eggs, or males with milt (which holds sperm cells and body fluids), but nearly all were dead or dying before spawning, and many were still in their ocean-phase colors, indicating that they had been in freshwater for a relatively short time.

Additional monitoring confirmed that the deaths weren't a one-time aberration. In 2002, the National Oceanic and Atmospheric Administration's (NOAA) Northwest Fisheries Science Center launched an ongoing investigation into coho spawner mortality, with key partners being Seattle Public Utilities, King County, and the US Fish and Wildlife Service. The study initially focused on coho returning to Longfellow and other urban creeks, which were then compared to coho in Fortson Creek, a well-forested tributary of the Stillaguamish River, north of Seattle. Fortson, which was surveyed in 2002, was fed by nearby streams and underground water flowing through a forest, and had a thriving coho run where pre-spawn mortality was virtually nonexistent. At Longfellow and other urban creeks, however, pre-spawn mortality was revealed as a common part of Puget Sound's landscape. (NOAA's research extends beyond stream surveys to include the probable impact of pre-spawn mortality on the region's wild coho populations, as well as the relationship between land use practices and coho die-offs, including how bioinfiltration systems like rain gardens can prevent pre-spawn mortality.) I had the best of intentions at Kelsey Creek, as I hope I did here at Longfellow Creek, but the results were far from what I wanted.

I heard a rustle in the leaves and glanced up from the grate to see a feral black cat dart into a Himalayan blackberry thicket. The call of *tikkun olam* can be just as weedy as such a thicket and even thornier, springing up everywhere, adapting to circumstances, evoking different meanings for different people. Whether reading the works of scholars, talking to rabbis or activists, or simply thinking back to my own efforts over the decades, I had yet to encounter a universally shared definition (or anything close to it) of what it means to repair the world.

Yet regardless of how tangled the thicket gets, the call to repair is genuine, arising from our best selves, I like to think, the part of all of us capable of acknowledging the harms we've created without shrinking away in guilt or fear. There's no end to the damage we've caused, just as there's no end to our curiosity, our capacity for good work, our intelligence, and our compassion. The reasons for despair are everywhere and profound. What's lost does matter. So does what's still here and what's still possible. Kelsey Creek offered one path away from the thorns. *Tikkun*, I've come to learn, isn't identified by intentions but by the impact of what we hope are reparative actions.

Glimpsing that impact requires a watchfulness that can take a lifetime or longer. Due to the large natural variability in the annual number of adult and juvenile salmon, some studies argue that minimally assessing the effectiveness of restoration techniques requires a decade or longer. Nature's time span can be far longer when it comes to restoring other species or ecosystems. Native conifers can take a century or so to mature, meaning that long-term impacts of forest restoration may not be known for decades. If restoration is a commitment to abundance in the future, then *tikkun*, in turn, is a commitment to humility in the present. It means returning time and again and observing anew, eyes open to what you'd perhaps rather not see.

Sitting on the cold stone above Longfellow's grate, I could only hope my citizen science efforts were helping to build that evolving knowledge. But what knowledge had I gained about science and citizenship? Should I clear this grate? I used to think clearing the grate would help reestablish a run, but I knew better now: even if I remove blockage to allow fish to pass, too many of the coho returning to Longfellow will die before spawning. While Longfellow Creek has some of the highest coho pre-spawn mortality rates among Seattle streams, in contrast, chum salmon appear immune to the toxic runoff, and they, too, mate in Longfellow and other local urban creeks. Even some Longfellow coho survive to spawn and die afterward as part of their natural cycle, becoming food for urban wildlife. While Longfellow's numbers are low, perhaps some young salmon do survive their year in the creek, eventually swimming downstream into Puget Sound. Some coho from Puget Sound streams spend their growing years there; others migrate out to feed and grow in the Pacific Ocean's coastal waters.

Once back at their spawning creeks, coho will be strong-bodied yet fragile, their immune systems shut down, their protein and fat reserves depleting. They will die as they have lived, unconcerned with us—even though their survival depends on human stewardship of creeks, rivers, estuaries, and the ocean. Is that why I cleared the grate? Was it for stewardship of the part of the watershed I touched as I sat on a concrete embankment? Was it for the relief of doing something? The satisfaction that what I did would some-how help? Or was that just a mask for pride? Was it to see coho at the footbridge? After all, why come here three days a week and pay attention if there's nothing to see? But I was there to observe data, not create it.

I pondered my questions. I shifted my position. No more grate-clearing.

Mid-October

A few weeks later, at the Southwest Yancy footbridge, a man in a green corduroy coat, with silver hair over stooped shoulders, gave me the fish gossip: "There won't be coho this early. Wait till Halloween. You'll see 'em holding under the footbridge before shooting upstream."

Later in the day, a thin elderly man walking a mud-splattered white poodle stopped to say that in the 1940s, the local fire station built a barn for its horses on Southwest Yancy. He pointed downstream, toward where I'd heard that beavers have tried to put in a dam, and said he remembered when the Duwamish came to a cove where the steel mill now sits.

"No silvers jumping in the river. Not yet," he said as he shook his head.

Coho at sea have silvery sides and a light belly—leading to their nickname of "silver salmon"—but in mating season their lower body turns wine-colored to gleaming bloodred, and they develop a pronounced red gill cover. Unlike these men stopping to talk with me at the footbridge, Longfellow's coho aren't necessarily local. They seem to be a mix of wild fish and strays from hatcheries or Puget Sound's tribal net pens. Straying behavior ensures that while most adult salmon return to natal creeks to spawn, a small number of adults will search out new habitats to colonize, thereby ensuring a population's continuance if a volcanic eruption or other natural disaster destroys a population's core freshwater habitat. Longfellow also has populations of rainbow trout, three-spined stickleback, and prickly and Pacific staghorn sculpins, all native fish, but sea-run cutthroat trout and steelhead are long gone.

"You're here too early," the old man said. Then he smiled and continued on his way.

Living fish. Dead fish. Courtship. A redd. What were the data I was watching for but a moment taken out of time, recorded, remembered? That old man's memories are data, a local knowledge gained from living decades in the same place. He drops his stories like seeds, planting them inside strangers. What does he hope will take root? If he doesn't pass his stories on, everything he's learned becomes just another lost bit of lore about a long-gone place, but the past is just that: a place that's gone, can't be changed, and is poorly remembered anyway. Sure, a place carries its history, but history isn't simply the past. History is the life lived right now. History is the story that life becomes in the future.

In the near future, though, I'd have my new home, the one created when Jim and I moved in together. It wasn't lost on me that now that I was finally ready to create a permanent home, Jim and I couldn't afford to buy a house in Seattle's hot, if not inflamed, real estate market. So we rented. We turned over soil in a backyard planting box long ignored by former tenants and an absentee landlord, put in compost, and planted seedlings of broccoli and tomatoes, raspberries and strawberries; we unpacked boxes, compared housewares, and cruised Ikea and Goodwill and yard sales for bookcases and bric-a-brac; we discussed whether one day we could afford to put an offer on our rented house with its double lot, incense cedar, wildly overgrown laurel and holly, and close proximity to good public schools. Then we compared our health insurance policies, and we realized that the window for adding me to Jim's policy at the University of Washington would close in November. So we got a marriage license, called our closest friends to be best man and matron of honor, and had a rushed wedding in our living room with a ceremony performed by a justice of the peace whom we never saw before and will never see again. And we waited to see if we'd been successful in creating the family we both want, just as I waited for another fish to head upstream or another passerby to cross the bridge and chat.

Behind these small, mundane actions was something larger than my new life with Jim. I realized now that my being at Longfellow was one way of living out a story to tell the child we hoped would soon be in our lives. I wanted our child to learn what a home is through our stories of how knowledge, work, stubbornness, and patience could bring a place back to as much life as it could still support.

Late October

Back again for another observation session, I reminded myself, *Whatever I see is important in its own right.* With each pencil mark, I would confirm that salmon were present at a stream site during a particular year and time of year. That thin line would reveal nothing about whether fish were present amid downed trees or in some other place where I couldn't see them. They might also be present at night (common during salmon migration) or after I leave. Still, putting citizen science data together gets you a working understanding of the general presence, location, and numbers of salmon in a given year. Assuming, of course, that I and the other volunteers see what's there, identify it correctly, mark it down, and do this session after session, year after year—so that the reliability and credibility of those lines write over nature's impermanence and memory's imperfections.

Nibbling at my still-positive attitude was the question, will this be a good day for fish? So far, it hadn't been. One fungus-chewed salmon circled upstream of the footbridge. Spots on its back and upper tail fin suggested that it was a coho, but if there were spots on the back and on both the upper and lower tail fin, it could be a Chinook. I couldn't see the fish's telltale gumline, so that was no help in identifying it. The fish shifted. Its spots appeared clearer, more distinct, and not blotchy like a Chinook's spots. I saw a red belly. I erased *unid* and marked down *coho*.

I watched and waited, and watched and waited. Sunlight sparkled on wind-rippled alder trees. Then what I first thought was a unid surged past the bridge and headed upstream, where females fight each other for access to redd sites, and males fight for access to females. A breeze across the downstream rush revealed the fish's red flash of belly and gill cover. I marked another *coho* on my monitoring form.

A fast-moving dorsal fin cut the creek and cast out ripples that fractured reflections of western redcedar, alder, and Pacific willow, and black-capped chickadees in flight. The fish was moving too fast to identify it, so I marked *unid*. I heard a tail slapping the water. Somewhere a female was digging her redd. Sunlight poured through the water, revealing a mosaic of stones and a salmon making its way upstream. Turned out to be a good day for fish after all.

JUST A FEW INCHES LONG, with a brown midsection and an orange-brown head and claws, I watched the creature glide over the streambed's silt and stones. My first crayfish! Are crayfish benthic indicators? Benthic invertebrates are bottom-dwelling stream creatures, such as insects, worms, or mollusks, and are good indicators of habitat and water quality, because they tend not to migrate, are sensitive to human impacts, and are easy to collect. Longfellow scores poorly for benthics, indicating its species diversity is poor and most likely made up of species that are short-lived, pollution-tolerant, or in other ways able to endure life in an urban creek. Watching the crayfish brought to mind more questions: Is it a native species? An invasive? Does Longfellow have a large population? Or is this creature at the vanguard?

Cottonwood leaves were turning gold. A grey sky promised rain. It was an ordinary day, but because of the crayfish, my mind was as open as my eyes. Now I had questions and questions and questions. Perhaps I was watching Longfellow not to see what was there but to see what wasn't yet known—to find questions, not answers. I remembered that beautiful thought from *Honey From Stone* by the astronomer and naturalist Chet Raymo: "Knowledge is an island. The larger we make that island, the longer becomes the shore where knowledge is lapped by mystery."

Every answer leads to questions; every question reveals a larger world; there are questions even in ordinary places. Maybe "mystery" is all the questions I would never have originally imagined. Maybe those unanticipated questions are what it means to see a place on its own terms.

Early November

Alder leaves fell with the rain. Three days of rain. Longfellow was running high and fast.

In the early twentieth century, Longfellow Creek flowed through a local wilderness. Rain fell on centuries-old cedar, spruce and Douglas firs, dripped upon snowberry, salmonberry, sword fern, and other shrubs, and sank into a welcoming earth, where it drained into Longfellow Creek, the Duwamish River, Elliott Bay, and other nearby waterways as fresh, cool groundwater. Now, roads, sidewalks and other impervious surfaces cover approximately half the city. Slightly over half of Longfellow's 2.7-mile watershed is made up of such surfaces, and almost the entire watershed drains into a system of pipes, storm drains, and other structures. Sixty-four storm drains shoot stormwater directly into Longfellow, while additional outfalls bring combined sewer overflows, a mix of stormwater and untreated wastewater, when severe storms overwhelm the pipe system.

Rain slides hard and fast off streets and sidewalks, picking up daily life's toxic droppings from pesticide and fertilizer residue from gardens, to gasoline, copper, arsenic, and lead, and a host of other metals that come largely from cars. (It's not lost on me that my driving to Longfellow adds to the creek's deteriorating condition.) One inch of rain water falling on a one acre parking lot can generate 27,000 gallons of stormwater that can pour into

Longfellow, or other creeks and waterways, and from there, flow out to Puget Sound.

Seattle is redesigning its drainage system to better control floods, stormwater runoff, and combined sewer overflows in the future, but on this day a middle-aged woman in a dark coat stopped as she walked across the footbridge and told me how high the water was the day before: three feet up the bank. We didn't know at the time, as we stared amazed at the rush of water pouring through Longfellow, but additional toxicology studies by NOAA would eventually show that when returning coho are directly exposed to stormwater runoff from city streets it can take as little as two and a half hours before the fish are dead.

The flood we saw that day was causing even more damage. It was eroding Longfellow's banks, digging gashes into the streambed, scouring out redds and smothering the embyros with silt, ripping out downed trees and other large woody debris, and pushing young salmon out of protective cover and into the waiting jaws of predators.

In this region, young coho typically spend a year in small freshwater streams before going to sea, although juvenile coho in British Columbia or Alaska could spend two years in freshwater. Their numbers are determined partly by the number of spawning adults, but also by a stream's length and its habitat quality, such as rearing pools containing large woody debris that can offer young fish a complex, sheltered instream environment where they can grow. These factors are harmed as cities expand into natural areas. Puget Sound coho have been labeled a "species of concern" and not listed as endangered, but in four of the region's river basins alone, increased urbanization has been matched to a 75 percent decline in coho.

Longfellow's instream habitat repairs couldn't offset the habitat-disturbing processes created by the surrounding developed landscape. And I had little hope of seeing any fish with the creek so fast and dark. Why not return to my warm car? Well, because even though I would never be a scientist no matter how many marks I made on a form, I would always be a citizen of where I live.

I've heard it said that people who restore urban streams have a "romantic relationship with muck." I tried to see past Longfellow's leaf-strewn rush as it washed away hard work and good intentions. I thought (or hoped) that my naïveté was also being swept away so that I could realistically assess what was still possible.

The *tikkun olam* needed to extend beyond Longfellow's physical habitat. The small acts of daily life were what brought on this roaring water. Are there mundane choices—walk rather than drive; vote; support a law or a lawsuit; rip out the concrete carport and in its place put in a rain garden, where soil and native plants can capture rain, prevent runoff, filter out pollutants, and slowly seep water into the ground—that can create an informed engagement with where we live? Like drops of water falling on a stone, can small persistent acts wear the rock away?

Late November

The afternoon light cast my pen's shadow on the page. Two salmon glided into view. The female cleared gravel with slaps of her tail, then went nose-to-nose with her mate before both disappeared as twilight darkened Longfellow's flow.

I glanced up. A great blue heron swooped down in long-winged grace to perch in an alder. What luck! A few minutes more, and I would never have spotted the bird amid darkness and branches. Only it wasn't luck. I've learned it's important to say thank you to this world for being here, but I can't do that without knowing what's here in the world with me. I used to think that meant learning to identify plants, birds, and other creatures, but Longfellow Creek contains another set of field marks. I'm learning to see those other ways of knowing home: the netting that holds the stream bank; the planted seedlings of western redcedar, spruce, snowberry, and Douglas fir; the trash hauled out; the graffiti painted over.

These and so many other ordinary, often anonymous acts balance the loneliness that I so often feel and that Aldo Leopold expressed in seeing ecological wounds. Discovering home means discovering you're not alone. Other people had come before me and left behind marks of repair and humility, reminding everyone who passes through of the harms of the past and the possibilities of the future.

It was getting dark. I shivered so badly that my pen jerked across the page. I put away my notebook. I drew my jacket close. I knew better than to think that all harms can be repaired. Yet alongside my loneliness I felt gratitude for the stubborn people who had loved and repaired Longfellow enough for a great blue heron to find shelter in the night.

December

I was cold under my polypro pants and jacket, cold under my hat and gloves, cold along my bones. I watched for fish. I saw rain plopping on the creek. I listened for splashing. I heard cars pounding streets. As November faded into December, I had seen chum and sometimes coho. But that had been a week or two back.

It was time to go home and mail in my data sheets. I would be back in the fall. While I am gone, Longfellow's flows would shift deadwood and gravel, and perhaps close old channels and open new ones. I dipped my hands in the creek and saw a salmon that was no more than tail and spine twisted over stone. I wanted something to feed me until I returned. What were those questions from September? Before there were citizens or science, there were people looking at the place where they lived, wondering: How did this fish get here? Why this tree? On and on it goes, until the question is revealed that's behind all the others: Why am I here? Organic farmer and poet Scott Chaskey wrote, "It is possible to replace the abstract question—why are we here?—with a local knowledge."

For years, I wanted a local knowledge to create a sense of home, as if a place could be analyzed like a prehistoric bee trapped in amber. My citizen science efforts have shown me that a local knowledge is never static or simple. Cities and streams, people and coho, even *tikkun*, change; no matter what we know, there is always more to learn about where we are and why we are here. The fun part is staying alert to what I still need to learn, to those unexpected creatures and unwanted moments, to ecological wounds, and to the resilience that illuminates this odd, lovely place.

I shoved my monitoring forms in my rucksack and walked up the trail. I would explore for just a little bit longer and then head home.

{ phinney ridge }

Early one January morning, awakened by the kicks and twists of my gestating daughter, I looked out the living room window, eager for a glimpse of a black-capped chickadee, a northern flicker, perhaps a great blue heron, cresting Phinney Ridge, my residential neighborhood. My daughter wanted to come into the world as much as I wanted to leave the empty days of doctor-ordered bed rest. For weeks now I had watched Jim head off to his work as a researcher in Alzheimer's disease and dementia at the University of Washington while I had lain flat on my back on the sofa. In the evenings, Jim went to book clubs or the weekly contra dances up the street while I, still on the sofa, waited for another day, another week, of pregnancy to pass.

At first, I thought I would like this quiet time. The solitude of my citizen-science sessions and nature explorations brought a necessary alertness to the landscape around me, a practice of informed attention all naturalists learn, which helps them glimpse the world's vastness and complexity. Stuck at home, however, solitude had narrowed my world—to my MacBook Pro, our wireless internet service, my books and writing notebooks, and my view from the living room windows. In a few minutes of release before I had to once again lie down, I looked past our barren rosebushes and searched the grey Seattle morning. I yearned for beautiful birds to enchant me, for wild birds to inspire me with their freedom to fly the world over, for native birds to remind me that my small home was part of a much larger place.

Instead, I saw starlings. I needed neither my binoculars nor my well-thumbed copy of the *National Geographic Field Guide to the Birds of North America* to identify those all-too-everyday nuisances. A flock of thirty or so of the small pointy-winged birds swooped between parked Saturns and SUVs, darted over my front yard's lavender, hovered above the rosemary bushes, and then clustered like gossiping sentries posted on the telephone lines.

I've heard more than a few bird-watchers call starlings "the sky rat" or "the weed with wings." And those are the nice things said about starlings. True, I'd had moments when I would admire the play of spots in a starling's plumage, or the flecks of green and purple along its glossy black wings. But mainly, when I wasn't ignoring starlings, I scorned them as pests. Or to be more scientific, I scorned the starlings as an invasive species.

Starlings aren't native to the United States but were released in New York City's Central Park in the early 1890s. In what sounds wacky enough to be an urban legend but, remarkably, isn't, Eugene Schieffelin and his compatriots from the American Acclimatization Society let loose some fifty pairs of starlings as part of a larger effort to bring to the United States all the birds mentioned in Shakespeare's plays and poems. Sixteen pairs of starlings are believed to have survived in their brave new world. Their descendants thrived. Eventually, starlings ventured beyond the city boroughs. Half a century later, starlings had spread across the country and reached the West Coast. Today, starlings can be found not just across the continental United States, but also large parts of Central America and the Caribbean. How many can trace their lineage back to those thirty-two avian pioneers? The far majority, it's believed, and possibly all of them.

I've seen my share of North America's estimated two hundred million or so starlings (thought to be approximately one-third of the world's starling population), in habitats as different as suburban backyards, city downtowns, and countryside fields. More than once, I've watched in amazement as gregarious chatterings (as the flocks are called), large enough to look like tens of thousands of birds, flew between the street trees of Seattle's Pioneer Square to old brick buildings in search of a twilight roost. Like many successful city birds, starlings eat a wide range of foods, from insects and earthworms to various berries, seeds, and garbage. As cavity-nesting birds, starlings can lay their eggs in the holes of an old tree snag as easily as in the gaps between an old building's brickwork or the eaves of a roof.

Though my Phinney Ridge house was far from Arizona's mountains, I could easily recall the moment in Erma Fisk's memoir, *The Peacocks of Baboquivari*, when she recalls seeing a pair of starlings near a southern Florida tool shed in 1965. She would later learn it was the first sighting of starlings so far south, and even decades later, she would lament not having " . . . wrung their necks. By the next year, the two had exploded to twenty, soon to sixty . . . When I left the area in 1978 there were hundreds . . . interfering with the native birds."

Fisk's sentiment is still a common one. Starlings can be aggressive birds and are believed to cause the decline of numerous native bird species, particularly by evicting other cavity-nesting birds from the holes needed for raising young. To examine this notion, scientist Walter D. Koenig's article "European Starlings and Their Effect on Native Cavity-Nesting Birds" drew on Christmas Bird

Counts and North American Breeding Bird Surveys to see if starlings had caused declines in approximately twenty-seven species of native cavity-nesting birds, including woodpeckers, sapsuckers, bluebirds, and one of my favorite raptors, the ever-so-lovely American kestrel.

With the possible exception of sapsuckers, Koenig concluded, "Native hole-nesting birds have thus far apparently held their own," and some might even be thriving, despite the all-too-abundant starlings. But if we can't dislike starlings for outcompeting native birds, we can find other reasons to want them gone, if only because starlings seem to be everywhere we look.

But that January morning, I forgot to dislike starlings. I certainly couldn't ignore them. The starlings alighted on front yards and pecked amid the winter-gold grass. They grounded themselves on earth, but I was aloft with joy. My bare feet tapped the wood floor. My imagination flew with the starlings through a sky of *what ifs* and *where to next*s, flying above our street of vine maple trees and white-trim homes, past the red-brick community center, and above the Starbucks. We took wing northward to the Skagit Valley, where we'd dodge red-tailed hawks and peregrine falcons, or journeyed eastward toward the farms of the Snoqualmie Valley. Or we might just fly and fly until we came to a place I'd never seen.

How was it that these mundane little birds were inspiring a stronger wake-up than anything in my morning cup of green tea? For just a few minutes, I wasn't bored out of my mind from the bed rest. Maybe that was why I was so happy at the sight of starlings, of all birds. But it was more than that, I knew, for I couldn't take my eyes from them. I was seeing them with what poet Leonard Nathan, author of the wonderful *Diary of a Left-Handed Birdwatcher*, calls "the electric experience when epiphany occurs, when hope or surprise meets intense presence," which brings the "knowledge of a meaning only intuitively grasped, of the wholeness of being."

Before this morning, starlings had been too everyday and ordinary to be an inspiration to me. Certainly ecological terms like *aliens, exotics, foreigners*, and similar labels used to describe nonnative species had helped to turn my eyes away from the starlings. That emotion-laden language of borders and boundaries has little to do with what an animal is—and everything to do with who controls the landscape: us or them. Poison or trap them, haul out the guns, and tear out their nest sites, the starling persists in claiming a space alongside us. Why not? Didn't all species evolve on Earth's common ground? Doesn't that give us an evolutionary kinship with all creatures, even starlings? After so many weekends at invasive plant removals, the Himalayan blackberry had earned my grudging respect. But could a weed be beautiful? An invasive inspiring? It was as if the frame of my window had shattered, leaving me with a wider view of home, and I could see the starling for the first time, as invasive nuisance yet wondrous creature.

The starlings rose. Their graceful flight took them around my neighbor's plum tree and away from our tabby cat. The starlings flew with the freedom all birds have to journey, to wander, to explore the vastness of our world, and to do it with the closeness of kin and companion. How I wanted that same freedom! Watching the starlings dash across roofs and between chimneys, I remembered what I'd forgotten in the boredom of the last few months. In just a few more weeks, I would have the freedom to lace up my shoes, open the front door, and go out into that big world. When I did, I would not be alone. My daughter would be exploring the world with me, one day seeing starlings for the first time, and someday reaching her own conclusions about these annoying, enchanting birds.

The starlings hovered, turned as one, flew up the street, crested the hill, and were gone.

{ the nisqually river }

"This will be the most disgusting thing you ever do," I warned my husband as we drove into Smallwood Park. During the two-hour drive south to the Nisqually River, first down I-5 from Seattle, then along the strip malls of State Route 167 and from there to the rural roads and open fields of State Route 161 heading into Eatonville, I'd kept my legs stretched across the Camry's backseat. It was a few weeks past Hanukkah, that time of light breaking the winter darkness, and I was in my second trimester of pregnancy and weeks past a threatened miscarriage that could have ended our daughter's life before it even started.

The high blood pressure that accompanied my pregnancy had meant I had to pull back from monitoring at Longfellow, and this was the first winter in years that I'd spent without a single trip to any other salmon stream. Except for medical appointments and rare outings, I'd spent my early pregnancy in a doctor-ordered, fear-enforced bed rest.

"I cleaned out the monkey cages when I was in graduate school," Jim said. With his brown hair and matching goatee, metal-rimmed glasses, and patched jeans, Jim looked less like the middle-aged man he was and more like the young graduate student he was in years past. "How bad could this be?"

Jim usually spent Saturdays running three miles, shopping at the farmers' market, and checking Medline for studies on high blood pressure during pregnancy. He knew I was stir-crazy from the bed rest. I yearned to be back in the literal woods and hoped we were out of the metaphorical woods of pregnancy disasters. The first trimester was over. My blood pressure was again normal. I knew this might be my last time outdoors once the baby arrived. What better way to spend it than by restoring a salmon run—even if it meant flinging fish carcasses.

For Jim, salmon restoration was more abstract than the data sets he analyzed as a research scientist. He didn't know that by returning to their natal streams, spawning salmon sustain hundreds of species—from mallards, which eat salmon eggs, to mergansers, which prey upon juvenile salmon, to seals and whales in the Pacific, which feed on immature salmon schools. Once the salmon are back in freshwater, eagles, shrews, and coyotes are but a few of the species that feed on the returning fish. In the Nisqually region alone, some 137 species of insects, mammals, and birds are fed through the annual return of salmon. Among the dozens of creatures attending the feast are the aquatic insects that will in turn be eaten by next season's juvenile salmon.

Myriad fish species also benefit. Bull trout and cutthroat trout will eat drifting salmon eggs that have been separated from the redd by the digging of later-arriving spawning female salmon, and many fish species will also eat the dead salmon, or the insects feeding on salmon carcasses. Even salmon benefit from their own deaths. Before migrating out to sea, juvenile salmon feast on the spawned-out carcasses, while juvenile coho will seek out salmon eggs during their freshwater phase. The larger a juvenile grows while in fresh-water, the greater its chances of surviving the winter, transitioning from smolt to adult, and eventually migrating downstream.

As in so many of the region's rivers, however, too few salmon were returning to sustain the Nisqually's flora and fauna. While estimates vary, one analysis of cannery records showed that the commercial harvest of salmon (south of British Columbia's Fraser River) peaked between 1882 and 1915, and estimated that historically 228 million to 351 million salmon returned annually to Alaska, British Columbia, and the Pacific Northwest during that time period, with 15 to 16 percent returning to what are now Northern California, Oregon, Washington, and Idaho.

Currently, only 1 to 1.5 percent of the estimated 142 to 287 million salmon produced annually return to these four regions, with the remainder returning primarily to Alaska but also to British Columbia. Fewer salmon means that Pacific Northwest streams are receiving a far smaller load of marine-derived nutrients than would have arrived with historically strong salmon runs. In the Puget Sound region, more than 75 percent of returning salmon are hatchery fish, not wild spawning fish, and for decades, hatcheries did not restore carcasses to rivers and streams.

The result is a sustained nutrient deficit, as it's called, which fish flings help rectify by seeding a river with salmon carcasses. Fish flings can't distribute the carcasses as widely across a river as would happen with natural spawning and, because the carcasses are spawned out, fish flings can't provide salmon eggs as a food source. By disturbing stream gravel during redd-building, naturally spawning salmon can help boost the numbers and kinds of stream invertebrates, an impact a fish fling can't replicate. Nonetheless, fish flings are a strategy proven to increase the number and overall size of juvenile salmon.

"This is something I never planned to do," said Jim as he maneuvered around SUVs to find a parking space. Smallwood Park was filled with families coming for the fish fling.

"Remember that C-section the doctors say is in my future?" I said. "If I complain about it, you can say, 'I drove sixty-odd miles so you could toss dead fish.'"

MY LEGS WERE STIFF as I stepped out of the car and started down a gravel road. Drizzling rain fell. The cold was a welcome contrast to my last fish fling several years before. That winter day had been oddly free of rain but abundant in sunshine—as well as buckets of ice-crusted dead Chinook and coho. By midday the ice had melted, and the fish had thawed to rotting flesh floating in bloody water. A nauseating stench had followed my group of fish flingers as we hurled carcasses into rivers and streams. Today, however, was cold. That cold would keep the fish frozen.

It might not be as bad as cleaning monkey cages, but I wasn't sure how Jim would deal with tossing dead fish. Or how I would. Before my pregnancy, I hiked mountain trails without a second thought. Now I worried I was pushing my luck walking a few hundred feet past picnic tables.

The road dead-ended. Coffee-drinking parents, their children swathed in raingear, stood beside pickup trucks. Nisqually Salmon Recovery Program staff grabbed carcasses from truck beds and tossed them alongside rear tires. Slick with ice slush and frozen blood, the coho were red-bodied in their spawning colors, while the Chinook were speckled with black dots along strong dark-green bodies. In rivers farther north of Puget Sound, young Chinook tend to stay in rivers and streams for a whole year. Most Puget Sound juveniles, however, will go to sea in their first year, typically in the late spring or early summer, although a few will stay an entire year in freshwater. This makes the species vulnerable to how humans alter river systems—whether from dam-building for hydroelectric power; urban development; or logging. In 1999, Puget Sound Chinook were listed as "threatened" under the Endangered Species Act, with habitat loss as one important reason. The Nisqually River—with its headwaters in Mount Rainier National Park, its lower tributaries protected from development by an army base and the Nisqually Indian Tribe's reservation, and its estuary in a wildlife refuge—emerged as a critical site for Chinook recovery.

The fish at our feet were born at Nisqually hatcheries and then released to migrate downstream to the estuary and then the ocean. Orange eggs smaller than a fingernail were stuck to a few carcasses. Some of the Nisqually's Chinook "stray" and spawn naturally, but most return to the hatcheries, where they are killed and gutted to remove eggs or milt for salmon production, and some are then frozen for fish flings.

Staff in weathered boots and raingear hauled shears out of the truck and started snipping off salmon tails so that biologists walking the Nisqually and its tributaries to count returning salmon could distinguish a fish-fling carcass from that of a naturally spawning fish.

"This little girl wants a small one," one father yelled out.

Chinook are the largest of the Pacific salmon, averaging thirty-six inches in length, nearly as long as some of the children were tall. Thinking about carrying a fish that big made me nervous. I yanked on plastic gloves and picked up a small coho.

Children raced past me up a hillock's muddy slope. I stopped. Before the pregnancy I would have raced with them. Now I was mired in *what ifs*: What if I slipped? What if I triggered a miscarriage? What if . . .

Weeks earlier, Jim and I had returned from the emergency room at 4 a.m., bleary with fear and sleep loss, clutching information sheets on threatened miscarriages. After that, my days had narrowed—no going up and down stairs, no sitting when I could lie down, no lying down without my feet up.

Maybe I should go to the car, I thought now. *Maybe that's too far. Maybe Jim should bring the car.*

But I remembered Jim saying in the days after the emergency room, "I can't live in this fear. I have to believe things will get better."

He meant this. He wouldn't be here with me at the fish fling otherwise, but he has stress lines in his cuticles and has been sleeping badly.

I took one slow, firm step. I was my father's daughter. I knew what a life defined by fear and illness was like. I knew, too, that my father would have loved a grandchild. But right now, what was before me was to take a slow, careful step, and another, and another. Finally, I arrived at the hillock's top. I looked down at the Mashel River, one of the Nisqually's tributaries, as it flowed downstream in a white-frothed rush.

In my years in the Pacific Northwest, I'd counted salmon, used them as sources of inspiration, and eaten them, of course. Yet I'd never touched one whole. I could feel the coho's strength, the heft of its body as melting ice softened its flesh. My gloves were slick with bits of salmon flesh. The coho almost slipped through my hands before I could throw it. It landed with a belly-up *plop* before sinking into the river's winter flow.

Fish soared through the air. Children ran back to the trucks, their parents barely having time to turn on their cameras before carcasses arced through the grey sky, smacked into swift water, and sank while children yelled, "Be free, fishy, be free!"

A boy held up to my face a jack, a small male that had left the ocean early to spawn. "This one was young when he died," he said before throwing it and running off to get another fish.

A pink-faced boy wearing a black fisherman's cap huffed through an underhand toss. "Sweet!" he yelled. Then he glanced at me, as if unsure that this stranger, this adult, could understand. I did.

A HALF HOUR LATER, our car caravan left the park. Two-lane black-top became a dirt road dead-ending at the confluence of the Nisqually and the Mashel. The rivers' torrent jammed deadfall against mossy boulders and broke against the concrete and metal remnants of a logging bridge.

Fish were tossed from the trucks onto gravel. "That one. I want that fish," children yelled. "Not that one. I want the other fish!"

Fear still stalked as close as my heartbeat. *I shouldn't be here*, I thought. *I should be home, feet up across the sofa.* But I was here. I walked where children ran. I veered around mud puddles they tore through. I felt my spirit sprint as I followed a Hansel and Gretel trail of orange salmon eggs scattered amid twigs, blood, and bits of flesh: a midwinter feast for the forest. I played—we all played—with death that stank and rotted and transformed into what fed the alder growing along the river, the eagle perched in its barren branches, the raccoons I suspected were waiting to scavenge carcasses once we left.

I tossed a coho from a spot alongside a girl in a Seattle Sonics jacket. She launched her Chinook with a full windup. Nearby, Jim was in a throwing contest with a brown-haired bespectacled boy who looked like his teenage doppelgänger. Other children argued over favorite *Star Wars* characters and whined for their iPods and electronic games, before at some point in the day cheering and throwing fish.

Coming back from the river, I passed a father with a salt-and-pepper beard, who stood before a clutch of preteen boys. "Look at this," he said, taking a coho and opening its belly, exposing veins, red organs, and pink flesh. Then he turned the fish toward the boys, stuck a wagging finger through its mouth, and said, "My name's Henry. What's yours?" The boys' eyes widened. Their jaws dropped.

I threw carcasses that thumped into conifer boughs and cracked against river rocks before slipping into the winter rush. With each toss, I felt joy as elemental as the fog forming from my cold breath. I remembered what fear had eclipsed: joy was why Jim and I were taking this hard journey toward having children. What's joy if not to move, to act, to create the world you want to live in? What was the point of having children if I couldn't pass along the simple, sustaining joy of restoring your home to abundant life? I laughed and walked, smelled sweet cedar, felt rain on my face and salmon in my hands, and threw fish after fish after fish.

By midday some five hundred carcasses were in the river. Back at the car, Jim said, "We'll do this again when our kid's old enough."

Isn't a tradition another kind of home, rooting us in our beginnings yet branching us out toward our future together? We couldn't have known that soon I'd be back on bed rest. Sooner than we'd hoped, our wonderful daughter would be born. Throughout those terrifying, chaotic days, I'd remember the fish fling as if it were a lodestar guiding me through the fear and flurry of her premature birth and my too-sudden motherhood.

"Sure," I said, stretching my legs across the backseat. "We'll be back."

{ the montlake fill }

Working my way along the cattails, seeking elusive bitterns along Lake Washington's shore, I discovered a homeless woman bundled in a stained brown sleeping bag. Her face was turned from the morning light. Auburn curls spilled across the damp black ground. Flanking her were cloth bags with woven cord handles, a maroon fake-alligator purse, and a torn khaki rucksack. I turned away. I didn't want to disturb her home when it already seemed as fragile as hummingbird wings.

I wasn't surprised to see her. The Montlake Fill is a refuge, and refuge is needed when home is gone. Nestled alongside the University of Washington's golf driving range and parking lots, and not far from an upscale shopping mall, the Fill's approximately seventy-five acres of wetlands, small ponds, and scattered woods provide sanctuary to painted turtles, rabbits, coyotes, and other assorted urban wildlife. Its tangled willows, muddy shores, and wind-stroked prairies shelter cedar waxwings and ruddy ducks, cinnamon teals and common yellowthroats. In her book *In My Nature*, master birder Constance Sidles, Seattle's local expert on the Fill, lists some 240 species of birds that have been seen there, including migratory ones flying between swiftly shrinking places to

.r another generation.

.nent is analogous to human life in Seattle, where

.nd rents are high and affordable housing is scarce.

Night Count, an annual winter census of Seattle

unty's homeless, reported 4,505 men, women, and

children ... ind living on the streets, a 19 percent increase over the previous year's count, and that didn't include the thousands of people living in overnight or emergency shelters, or in transitional housing programs.

What makes good habitat for a green-winged teal? It's a short list: food, shelter from the elements, and protective cover from predators. What makes a refuge for a homeless woman sleeping beside cattails? Any place where she won't be raped, or robbed, or pissed upon. Any place where she won't be seen unless she wants to be seen. While the One Night Count usually finds homeless people in cars, beneath overpasses or other urban structures, or simply walking with nowhere to go, there are always people seeking refuge in public parks. When I told a friend about finding the homeless woman at the Fill, he mentioned the half year he spent living in a plastic lean-to within a greenbelt. Nature's the home where the door's always open.

The Fill wasn't always a refuge. For a long time, the Mont-lake Fill was the Montlake Landfill, a garbage dump along Lake Washington's Union Bay. The riparian, or streamside, ecosystems of Yesler Creek, Kincaid Ravine, and Ravenna Creek used to join at Union Bay, where the Fill now sits. Construction of the Ship Canal and the Chittenden Locks, completed in 1917, caused Lake Washington to drop by approximately nine feet and in places exposed what was once lake bottom. The resulting Union Bay site, a mix of marsh, swamps, mudflats, and peat bogs, which was owned by the University of Washington, was leased to the city of Seattle

and infilled with dirt and rubbish. And while historical source
vary, the Fill apparently had opened to public dumping by the
mid-1920s. Everything from household garbage to construction
rubble found its way to the site, with sometimes more than a hundred truckloads arriving daily.

By the mid-1960s, garbage disposal there began to end, and
some portions of the landfill were converted to parking lots and
playing fields while other areas were graded, covered with clay
and soil, and seeded with grass. Black cottonwood and other
native trees colonized the wetter edges, but most of the Fill became
overgrown with purple loosestrife, Scotch broom, Himalayan
blackberry, and other invasive plants. In the mid-1970s, the University of Washington's Center for Urban Horticulture began
planning the Fill's restoration as a living laboratory for field classes
and critically needed habitat for birds and wildlife in an increasingly developed city. Actual restoration began in 1990.

I discovered the Fill in the late 1980s. When I first moved to
Seattle, I was eager to get out and explore the Pacific Northwest's
legendary natural beauty, but other than the nearby national parks,
I didn't know where to find its wild places—much less recognize
what was living there. The Montlake Fill was a quick and easy excur-
sion. When tight schedules or other demands kept me in the city,
I could still sneak in a few twilight hours or early morning walks
at the Fill.

I remember walking boot-trampled foot trails through knee-
high grass, rambling past seemingly impenetrable swatches of
Himalayan blackberry, becoming more and more lost from my
mundane worries and expectations, certain only that I never knew
quite what or who I would encounter. One afternoon, when it
had required stout boots and extra socks to navigate the rain-
sodden ground, I reached a winter pond; there I found a short

s

man with a European accent, his battered binoculars
m a tattered strap. He told me of the snowy owls he had
at the Fill, fell silent, and left. I never saw him again.

different winter day, when Lake Washington had frozen
s shorelines, I looked past mergansers and gadwalls toward
uses along the other side of the bay. There I saw a man
sed in plaid knickers, his red scarf twirling down to his waist,
he performed pirouettes on ice skates, spinning his way into my
memory.

On some rambles, I jumped back as ring-necked pheasants
exploded out of the silver winter grass. Other times, I spied northern harriers or short-eared owls flying low, circling patrols over
tawny fall grass. I learned to bird watch at the Fill. But what I really
learned was to stay alert for beauty in overlooked places.

A season would shift, and the refuge would be a home to a new
group of birds. In the winter, I watched green-winged teals and
ruddy ducks glide atop ponds created by the heavy rains. If I was
lucky, I'd find dunlins, occasional refuge visitors, as a fast flock
flashed in sunlight's glint. In spring, western sandpipers and least
sandpipers skittered along the ponds' receding edges. The smaller,
rain-fed ponds dried out with the summer, and protective flocks of
Canada geese herded awkward goslings over the damp earth. There
were many times when the only birds I saw were the year-round
killdeers, crows, or mallards.

Sometimes the fall and winter rains left sizable ponds that lasted
until spring. Other years the Fill was dry. Regardless of its changes,
the refuge's endless appeal was in being scraggly and obscure, a wild
place hidden in plain sight, within a short walk to grocery stores
and Chinese restaurants.

I think the homeless woman sleeping alongside the cattails
needed the Montlake Fill for much the same reasons I did. She

had practical reasons, of course, for the Fill is a few blocks from the University District's bus lines, food banks, and small stores that might use workers for odd jobs. Maybe she needed the Fill's close proximity to domestic violence programs and emergency shelters. I've met the people who prove what local and national statistics show year after year—namely, that physical or sexual violence in the home is a leading cause of homelessness for women and children. Perhaps the woman sleeping in the cattails needed the Fill more than most—if only because it's better to wake to birdsong than to footsteps in an alley. When all you have left is what you carry, beauty still beckons in the sunlit brilliance of an American goldfinch; it reminds us of a world larger than our lives.

THE FILL WAS WHERE I learned the names of some of my neighbors: yellow warbler, common merganser, green heron. But other neighbors kept their names to themselves. One day, while watching fast-moving flocks of white-crowned sparrows, I came upon a narrow, curving path that led into what seemed to be an impenetrable Himalayan blackberry thicket. Curious about where it went, I crouched low to escape the thorns and scuttled into a verdant cavern. Sunlight edged between stalks that had been cut away to form walls and a roof. Somewhere in those open walls, cedar waxwings chattered in glorious abandon. Worn blankets lay on the ground. Faded plaid shirts were strung on lines across the stalks. Shoes were beside the entrance. Yellow coffee mugs, battered tin camping pots, and rain-soaked cardboard boxes were placed neatly nearby.

Why, I'm in someone's home, I thought. I felt rude, as if I had just barged into someone's living room. Maybe I had. Maybe the man who lived in the blackberry thicket was one of the working poor, someone whose wages were too low to afford market-rate housing, and who planned to make his home at the Fill until he had the money, friends, or good luck to move on. The ground might be cold, and the rain might drizzle through the ceiling, but the Himalayan blackberry's thick square-edged stalks, jagged leaves, and sharp thorns created a botanical shelter concealing the homeless man from predators or passers-by, and its purple-black berries gave sustenance. Protection and sweetness—isn't that what makes a home?

I backed away from the broken plates and mottled sunlight. I hadn't been invited to enter. I didn't return.

BY THE EARLY 1990S the Fill started to lose its scraggly obscurity. Habitat restoration began with the removal of invasive plants like purple loosestrife. As the years passed, I found myself on fewer boot-tramped footpaths; instead, a gravel loop trail guided my steps to certain places and not others. Of course, this kept me (and many others) from inadvertently crushing the eggs of ground-nesting birds or accidentally chasing off migratory birds that needed food and rest before their next round of flight.

Interpretive signs began to spring up, and while they were informative, additional signs appeared nearby that read Do Not Enter. Restoration in Progress. Then at some point, people started calling the Fill by its formal name: the Union Bay Natural Area.

I couldn't argue with these changes and still can't. I disliked the new name and still do, but I had to admit it was more accurate to the place. Garbage dumping had ended decades ago. Now the landscape was increasingly designed for birds and wildlife, and unarguably those changes made the place not just more natural but also more wild. Yet the more natural the Fill became, the more artificial it appeared to me, with borders to my wandering and barriers to my wondering.

Sometime between my visits, the homeless man's blackberry-bush refuge disappeared. In its place there was an experimental planting of dewberry, thimbleberry, snowberry, and other native plants. These names were sweet with history. These were among the native plants that had provided food and shelter to resident and migratory birds before wetlands, forests, and other natural areas were taken down to build suburban developments or condos with Puget Sound views.

I can still feel my loyalty split. *Tikkun olam* offered no clear, easy answers—it never does. It never will. I've seen both ecological restoration and social justice advocated under its call, but that day, abstract ideals shrank to a practical question: Which of my neighbors needs a home more?

My curiosity for where the man who lived in the berry bushes went was, in the end, stronger than my compassion. He went somewhere, and I hoped it was to a better place. But for birds, homelessness is called *habitat loss*, a euphemism for displacement that, if severe, can lead to extinction. In 2007, the National Audubon Society's *Common Birds in Decline: A State of the Birds Report*, listed twenty species that had lost 50 percent or more of their population since the late 1960s. A tally appearing in a Seattle Audubon newsletter found that fourteen of those species were regularly found in Washington State. Some were occasionally found at the Fill, such as the American bittern, the greater scaup, and the loggerhead shrike.

There are many reasons why bird populations are declining, including pesticides, but especially kills by domestic cats. Cats, either feral or pets, kill some 1.4 billion to nearly 4 billion birds yearly, and those are just the estimates for the continental United States (not counting Alaska and Hawaii, and of course not counting Canada or Mexico), causing noted ornithologist John Marzluff to write, "One in every ten birds in the United States will see the same thing just before death: a cat." Yet another core reason for bird declines is habitat degradation and loss including the spread of urban areas.

Urbanization's impact on birds is a complex and evolving subject, but the classic paradigm has long been that the less "disturbed" (developed) a habitat is, the more bird (and other) species will be found there. Cities preferentially favor a handful of bird species by fracturing forests, wetlands, and other native habitats into isolated areas interspersed with roads, buildings, and other human-oriented urban land cover. The more urbanized the landscape becomes, the fewer the number of bird species, largely because cities cause green spaces with an abundant variety of native plants to be torn up for buildings and pavement, or replaced by a small number of plants—primarily ornamental, often exotic or invasive flora, such as English ivy—which don't offer diverse bird species the food, shelter, or other ecological services they need to survive. The *number* of individual birds in a city can increase, however, as its skies will fill with massive flocks of starlings, rock pigeons, house sparrows, and a handful of other species, many of them nonnative, that make themselves at home in human-dominated environments.

Often these will be seed-eating or ground-foraging species, or else the generalist "weedy" species that are able to adapt to a wide range of habitats, from prairies to city parks, and able to eat foods ranging from seeds to insects to sandwich ends. These synanthropic species, including crows, gulls, and other avian compatriots that have a long and successful history of associating with humans, are often disliked, considered pests (or worse), or ignored for being an all-too-everyday part of the landscape. Which, come to think of it, is the same response many people have when encountering a homeless person.

Cities also tend to be good habitat for hawks, falcons, and owls, especially the smaller raptors that can live in parks. There's always another pigeon to eat, not to mention an abundance of small birds and mammals. Although it was years ago, I can still remember the lucky thrill of seeing a Cooper's hawk streak above the Fill in hot pursuit of a Steller's jay that was flying fast into a copse of trees. Branches shook. Birds shrieked. An aggrieved hawk screeched out of the trees and took off in search of easier prey.

In that classic paradigm, though, over time a city's bird species were believed to become quite different from the native bird communities that remained in nearby remnant natural habitats, and more similar to the bird species found in cities hundreds or thousands of miles away.

In 2014, a global study of the birds found in 54 cities and flora found in 110 cities (located across thirty-six countries found in six continents and six biogeographic regions), published in the *Proceedings of the Royal Society B*, alternately upheld and upended that paradigm. When looking at bird species density (as measured by the number of species per kilometer), the study showed that cities across the world shelter far fewer species than do nonurban areas. To no one's surprise, rock pigeons, house sparrows, European starlings, and barn swallows were the "cosmopolitan" birds found in more than 80 percent of the cities studied. What was surprising, though, was that at least on a global level, cities are far more diverse in their bird and plant species than previously suspected.

Some 2,041 bird species (20 percent of the world's more than 10,000 bird species) reside in cities, and by and large, these birds are native to their region. When flora was tallied, cities also harbored significant number of species that hailed from the local bioregion (although again, nearby natural areas contained more native plant species than urban areas). Even more remarkable, cities around the world are sheltering birds and plants considered at risk of extinction according to the International Union for Conservation of Nature (IUCN) Red List. The classic inverse relationship, though, between species diversity and a city's human-oriented environment still held: the more urban land cover, the less vegetation and the fewer bird species flying across its skies. This makes conserving or restoring a city's flora a critical way of keeping diverse birds in the landscape.

Closer to home this dovetails (no pun intended) with urban ecology research from John Marzluff and his colleagues at the University of Washington showing that while the "fab five" urban birds (starlings, house sparrows, mallards, Canada geese, and rock pigeons) are all too common, nonetheless "the peak in bird diversity occurs where the creative hand of urbanization surpasses the destructive hand." Examining bird surveys conducted at one hundred urban, suburban, and forest settings in and around Seattle showed that the number of bird species was slightly higher in forests than in cities, but highest in the suburbs. What Marzluff calls *subirdia* is a geographic tapestry of adjacent residential, commercial, and natural areas that create a mix of savanna-like lawns, small forests, and a host of other microhabitats. Subirdia's habitat diversity opens the door for a wide range of bird species to move in and thrive. Moderate development, where flora remains diverse and urban land cover comprises half or less of the landscape, means food is abundant and readily available, ranging from fruits to nuts to insects and other invertebrates, not to mention the tons of seeds humans put in bird feeders.

Subirdia occurs in temperate zones, not the tropics, and while the suburbs are the heart of subirdia, also important are a city's flora-filled school or hospital campuses, its business parks alongside (or designed to re-create) forest reserves, its golf courses (if built in an already-developed area and if native vegetation is retained), its cemeteries, and of course, its parks and open spaces, like the Fill.

Subirdia has an ever-changing kaleidoscope of bird species, most of which are native to their bioregion, and which Marzluff and others delineate as avoiders, exploiters, and adapters. Some species have such specific habitat needs that they're forced to drop out of increasingly developed areas (such as hairy woodpeckers, which need the dead trees common in forests but rarely tolerated in the suburbs). The fab five and other cosmopolitan birds exploit even our most human-oriented landscapes.

Other bird species are adapters boasting an evolutionary repertoire that lets them take advantage of the new habitats created by fires and other natural disturbances, an ability that transfers easily when a forest is cut into patches interspersed with a suburb's open, grassy stretches and small shrubs. The number and variety of avoider, adapter, or exploiter species changes over time as a landscape changes from natural habitat to moderately developed to highly developed, and perhaps changes yet again if restoration diversifies flora and habitat.

The Fill's landscape changes left me grumbling, but they were what was needed to help keep more bird species local than just the fab five. Little wonder then that the Union Bay Natural Area and Shoreline Management Guidelines describes restoration as "an extension of conservation; it is what you do to protect the environment when there are fewer and fewer surviving natural systems to conserve."

My dilemma remains: Himalayan blackberry bushes for a homeless man or dewberry bushes for a cedar waxwing? I want thimbleberry and affordable housing, red alder and a sustainable economy. I want a city and a world big enough for all of us.

AT SOME POINT, weeks and then months and finally years slipped by between my visits to the Montlake Fill. As my skills as a lay naturalist and hiker grew, I wanted to see places that were more challenging to explore, more pristine, and farther away. I think those early years rambling at the Fill sensitized me, so that when I went out to the Cascades or the Olympic Mountains, or along the coast and shoreline or into the lowland forests, I was more alert than I would otherwise have been. I could trust that a wild beauty was there. I would see it if I were patient and knowledgeable.

I had the freedom then to wander to those far-off places because I wasn't yet married and didn't yet have a child. Everything changed once more when my daughter, Arielle, was born. Time, which had once been as common as a penny, became as guarded as a miser's gold. I thought I needed time. What I really needed was a chance to shake up assumptions and get lost from what I thought I knew, to wander by foot and ramble by mind, to open my eyes to more than feeding schedules, diaper changes, Arielle's next pediatrician's appointment, all the dull demands of daily life narrowed to one small home. I knew that, at best, I'd have only an hour or two, and only now and then, for getting out of the house. That was when I remembered the Fill.

But the Fill was no longer the place I recalled. I went back late on a rainy July Fourth afternoon nearly a year and a half after the tumult of Arielle's premature birth. Birds tweeted and trilled across the darkening sky. I left Wahkiakum Lane and walked toward one of the ponds. I stopped. A landmark was missing. Gone were the tumbled concrete blocks that had sheltered a covey of California quail. Walking back to the lane, I continued on to Wahkiakum Prairie and saw that where there used to be labyrinths of Himalayan blackberry were now native camas, slender cinquefoil, Roemer's fescue, sweet vernal grass, and other grasses. The Himalayan blackberry had given protective cover to breeding colonies of pheasants and California quail, and I later learned that both species had become extirpated at the Fill as the blackberry was removed, although an occasional lone bird is sometimes sighted or heard.

The cattails were still along the Lake Washington shoreline, and between stands of red alder, Pacific madrone, and other newly planted native trees were easy strolls to winter ponds that in the past had been barricaded by Himalayan blackberry brambles or ankle-sucking mud. There were fewer places to sleep hidden away. I suspected the homeless were still around, at the margins of sight. I hoped this new Fill offered them more than shelter.

My memories of the Fill seemed as thick as Himalayan blackberry, all sharp thorns and sweet berries. This new Fill's neat trails were disappointingly tame. I walked deep in mundane thought, tramping amid worries of unpaid bills, dusty rooms, unanswered messages, and dirty laundry. Then I glanced down and saw that amid dandelions and white daises were waves of purple flowers. I should have known that flower. I didn't. I made notes on its petals and other attributes that I could check against field guides when I got home, and continued on, but I was soon worrying about when I would be able to restart my grant writing business and ruminating on the cost of nannies.

Then the trail took me to where a parking lot was supposed to be. Had it been so long since my last visit that I'd simply forgotten how the trail worked? Or did trees and grasses truly reclaim what had once been tire tracks and gravel? I stood still. I didn't know where I was, but I knew I was where I needed to be, surprisingly and pleasantly lost.

A yellow bird with black wing tips rose and dipped as it flew past me to forage on the trail. A Wilson's warbler? Or an American goldfinch? I'd forgotten a lot in the last few years, caught up in home, marriage, and family. It wasn't just the Fill's landscape that had changed in my long absence. The birds and wildlife were also different. I'd never been good at identifying the birds that were drawn to the Fill's expanded grasslands and nearby forested areas. This was my chance to learn. But I'd have to set aside my nostalgia. This new Fill could only be seen with open eyes, open ears, an open heart. I hauled out binoculars and a birding field guide, and started exploring.

Soon enough, I found a stand of ivy-strangled trees near a pond. I remembered another day's walk from years before, when a rainstorm had broken, dark and brief as a tantrum. I had ducked into this grove. The trees' canopy had made a fluttering barrier from the rain. Thick, gnarled roots had surfaced only to plunge back into the ground. A Coke can had been half-hidden amid the ivy, and there had been pink graffiti on a tree trunk too wide for me to wrap my arms around. I remembered seeing a great blue heron standing on a log along the shore, the bird's plumes fluttering in the wet wind, its long legs thin, still lines in the storm.

That long-ago day rambling through the Fill and so many days like it, had seasoned me for the longer walk of discovering that home isn't an accident of birth or death any more than it's a way station or a past refuge. "Home is a den, a burrow, a cave, a cottage, a nest, a treetop, a room, a penthouse, a pond, an ocean, a meadow, a set," wrote Scott Chaskey. The Fill was a home, yes, but I've come to believe something somewhat different from Chaskey. What did my explorations through the Fill and so many other places show me but that *home* is not a noun, a solid unchanging place we find once and for all. We create home with each action we take, all the while learning why we're here and how we're to live in a place with all its bleakness and beauty, its paradoxes and pleasures. For home can be many places yet is the same place, the one that makes no promises, takes years or a lifetime to understand, and changes us as we change it.

Thinking back to that long-ago day amid these trees, I'm sure I thought that soon enough, I'd need to be on my way. What I remembered, though, is that I leaned back and stayed for a time, sheltered in a nest of tangled roots.

{ green lake park }

By the time the daffodils are in bloom and the red-winged black-birds are setting up their nests in Green Lake's cattails, the turtles emerge from their underwater dens, or out from under stumps and logs, to bask in the spring sunlight. The return of turtles means that spring is bursting out of Seattle's winter and into sunlight, so bright I have to buy sunglasses to make up for the ones I inevitably lose during seven months of grey skies and rain. Shortly after the turtles emerge come other small celebrations, such as the return of bumble bees to my lavender bushes, the opening of farmers' markets, and the planting of tomato, basil, and strawberry seedlings in my garden. As George Orwell wrote in his essay "Some Thoughts on the Common Toad," "the pleasures of spring are available to everybody, and cost nothing."

To these springtime joys, I can now add the birth of my daughter, Arielle. She arrived three months too soon and spent her first spring in an incubator at the University of Washington Medical Center's Neonatal Intensive Care Unit (NICU). She managed to be born the day after the vernal equinox, and in a befuddling stroke of coincidence on a day that was simultaneously Good Friday and the first day of the Jewish holiday of Purim, which celebrates an unexpected liberation from what could have been disaster. No matter how you look at it, spring is her season. Maybe turtles will become her sign of spring.

Early in the spring I could expect only two or three red-eared sliders, perhaps four, atop logs tethered to Green Lake's northwestern corner. It's a busy part of the city park, near Aurora Avenue and its many lanes of traffic, but the turtles seem as indifferent to the roar of cars as they are to the people who stop walking the lake path to count them. The turtles' necks are typically extended, showing yellow stripes and a red slash just behind each eye. Their legs are in a sturdy four-point stance, their carapaces weathered to a dark green, but even at a distance I can occasionally catch a glint of their bright-yellow undersides.

Red-eared sliders are the "dime-store turtles," popular pets that are also nonnative to the Pacific Northwest. Among Green Lake's turtles is Red Dragon, named by a tenant in my old apartment building who had rescued the turtle from neglect by a grade-school science class. When the tenant later moved to Virginia, Red Dragon moved to Green Lake. There it found a breeding colony of other red-eared sliders, most likely also abandoned pets.

Pet abandonment is a common way that red-eared sliders enter new areas. Once in place, they compete with native turtles for food, and basking and nest sites. They also spread respiratory diseases and other illnesses acquired from unsanitary conditions in the pet trade. Washington State has two native, freshwater turtles, the western pond and the painted turtle. The former has declined due in part to loss of habitat and introduced predators such as bullfrogs, but the painted, which is found throughout the state, was introduced into the Puget Sound region in the 1950s and 1960s, and is commonly seen at the Montlake Fill and other green spaces near lakes.

Red-eared sliders, like all turtles, are some of our world's great survivors, heirs to an evolutionary lineage extending back more than two hundred million years. Individual turtles are remarkably long-lived, due to a range of adaptations that include body shells capable of withstanding attack. Despite predators ranging from raccoons to coyotes, dogs, eagles, and all too often automobiles, red-eared sliders can live for an impressive quarter century or longer.

Come summer, there will be two dozen or so red-eared sliders on the logs. By then, there will be red-winged blackbirds trilling in the cattails, purple irises blooming by the lakeshore, and Himalayan blackberry vines shining with new leaves. But early in the spring Green Lake's turtles are almost as solitary and certainly as unremarkable as the common toad George Orwell wrote about. For Orwell, the common toad, the cuckoo, and the blackthorn were among the many small yet vibrant creatures and plants that heralded spring and its pleasures. When "Some Thoughts on the Common Toad" was published in 1946, the world's long winter encompassed the international depression of the 1930s, the rise of Fascism and Nazism, and the horrors of World War II, including the blitz of England. If hope was hard to come by, Orwell found signs of spring in the everyday resilience of nature, regardless of what we do to ourselves or to our world: "a brighter blue between the chimney pots or the vivid green of an elder sprouting on a blitzed site . . ." And he took great pleasure in the return of spring: "Every February since 1940 I have found myself thinking that this time Winter is going to be permanent. But Persephone, like the toads, always rises from the dead at about the same moment."

I discovered "Some Thoughts on the Common Toad" a few weeks after the Nisqually fish fling, when I was once again on bed rest but still hoping for a summer delivery and wondering if I'd be able to resume salmon monitoring in the fall, perhaps with Arielle snuggled close to my chest. I took my medications, saw my doctors, and reminded myself that soon, soon, one day soon Arielle and I would be discovering local birds, walking along streams, and exploring our world together.

I thought of Orwell's essay often the spring my daughter was born. It would be narcissistic to compare one difficult pregnancy and a resulting premature birth with the overflowing misery of Orwell's era, the suffering on a global scale that came on top of the unavoidable load of adversity every person encounters. But after my winter of threatened miscarriages, rocketing blood pressure, bed rest, and an emergency hospitalization followed by a cesarean section, Orwell's words resonated. He reminded me that more than half a century ago, the world's long winter was also a time of courage and persistence, and that from the ashes of an old world a new one arose. Even now, I try to remember that when I think of the world Arielle will inherit, one facing climate change and other environmental disasters, one that still needs our courage and persistence.

I imagine that the spring rebirth that Orwell watched for happened around the time of the vernal equinox, when, as he said, "the sooty privets have turned bright green, the leaves are thickening on the chestnut trees, the daffodils are out . . . and even the sparrows are quite a different colour." If spring could be found in the small ordinary signs of a world in rebirth, then it seemed to me that hope was also there. After all, if you can't find hope in what's small and everyday, where can you find it?

Of course, turtles are also small and ordinary, and, just as Orwell wrote of the common toad, "never had much of a boost from poets." Some two months after Arielle finally left the NICU and came home, a message from the *Writer's Almanac* landed in my email inbox with a poem entitled "Turtle" by Kay Ryan, who wrote: "Who would be a turtle who could help it? / A barely mobile hard roll, a four-oared helmet . . . Her only levity is patience, / the sport of truly chastened things." Hardly the description most folks would give to an icon of spring.

Most springs, I stopped to look for turtles during my daily walks around Green Lake. But the spring of Arielle's birth, I only glimpsed the turtles from a distance as I drove north along Aurora Avenue and happened to look out the window at just the right tree break along the shore. Arielle's birth weight was one pound, eleven ounces, and she didn't look more than a tad larger than the red-eared sliders in the lake.

I went to the NICU daily that spring, staying from midmorning until early evening. I took Arielle out of her incubator for an hour of skin-to-skin ("kangaroo") contact, changed her diaper, recorded her temperature, checked her medical logs, pumped breast milk seven or eight or nine times a day, and talked with endless rounds of nutritionists, physical therapists, nurses, residents, and attending physicians. I looked beyond Arielle's incubator and saw a ward full of incubators, and beyond that, ward after ward of incubators, each incubator cradling a new life, some struggling to survive. I thought of the streams run dry I'd seen, the littered and weed-covered riparian zones, the world that was once simply beautiful but now needed our imagination and dedication to bring its beauty back.

The longer Arielle was in the hospital, the more I read about the medical risks of prematurity. I had nightmares. Arielle was small but stubborn. She managed to avoid so many complications common to micropreemies—brain hemorrhages, lung dysfunctions of one kind or another, retinal damage that could lead to full or partial blindness, cerebral palsy, infections that lay waste to the intestines—but despite her good luck, it took nearly eleven weeks before Arielle could reach a solid weight, regulate her body temperature, and eat fairly regularly from a bottle.

Spring that year became sunlight streaming between hospital blinds; the smell of antiseptic soap; the beeps and clicks and alarm bells of oxygen saturation and heart rate monitors; the chatter of strangers in elevators, hallways, and cafeterias; and the not-so-whispered conversations doctors had with parents about relapses, risks, and the great unknown of life beyond the hospital. Outside the hospital and closer to earth than the sixth-floor NICU, the days lengthened and brightened, and I took it on faith that somewhere there were young salmon emerging from stream gravel, daffodils blooming, bumble bees buzzing, and turtles basking, their legs and necks stretched to catch the sunlight.

We had more questions than answers when we finally brought Arielle home. Had we missed a catastrophe? Was something lurking in her future, perhaps developmental delays or other struggles that would become apparent as she grew older? What future could she have, especially growing up in a world so damaged? All our questions were really just one: Could we feel hopeful?

What had I learned at Cottage Lake Creek, at Longfellow Creek, at Ellsworth Creek, at plant salvages and weeding sites and other small places of stubborn repair, if not that hope isn't optimism or certainty or any other feeling, really. Hope is the action you take, no matter how small or slow, to lead to a better end.

I can't say I'd ever been particularly interested in turtles before Arielle's birth. I enjoyed seeing them at Green Lake or Longfellow, but otherwise never thought of them until the spring Arielle was born, when I reminded myself of how the turtle's slow, steady step has trod along hundreds of millions of years of life on Earth. Few creatures can claim such an impressive lineage of survival. Small to the point of insignificant, beneath our gaze and underfoot, slow, steady, unnoticed —that's how most people think of turtles, I suppose. But the spring of Arielle's birth, I thought of turtles as creatures for the long haul, when much is unknown, when the important thing is simply to take that next step, and the next, and the next.

Her first spring, Arielle lay snuggled in fleece blankets in her incubator. Her second spring, I wheeled Arielle in her stroller around Green Lake to show her turtles. Turtles, cattails, red-winged blackbirds, daffodils—it was all the same to Arielle, all part of a big world she had yet to discover.

As Orwell wrote, ". . . Spring is still Spring. The atom bombs are piling up in the factories, the police are prowling through the cities, the lies are streaming from the loudspeakers, but the earth is still going round the sun, and neither the dictators nor the bureaucrats, deeply as they disapprove of the process, are able to prevent it."

So many decades after Orwell wrote of common toads, the bombs are still piling up, the lies are still streaming, and new dangers like climate change are here. Is it wrong or naive—or simply stupid or impossible—to enjoy spring in the face of so many harms we've done to our world? That's pretty much the response I've gotten when telling people about the turtles, and judging from the daily emails I get from environmental groups, it's as if all we can be feeling is anger, guilt, and fear. Those messages have moved me to give money, sign petitions, send letters in support of legislation or policy changes, talk to lawmakers, register voters, and cast my own vote. But it's not why I change my habits, or give my time or energy in ways I hope will restore the world I live in, the world Arielle will inherit. For me, and I think for most people, the courage and persistence to do that comes from the everyday gratitude of knowing turtles, toads, or whatever nature graces our small corner of the world.

Unlike her mother, Arielle was born in this place I've learned to call home. She's a Pacific Northwest native, and she'll have her life ahead of her to decide what this place means to her. Will she call it home? Or will she be called to do some wandering of her own? Those are big questions, and ones for another day.

Orwell's right, after all. Spring is still spring. Arielle is healthy and growing. Turtles are sunning on logs. I'm going to enjoy it.

{ **acknowledgments** }

There are a lot of people to thank for their unwavering encouragement in seeing *Turning Homeward* make its way into print. I especially want to thank Waverly Fitzgerald for her friendship, extensive publishing expertise, and excellent editorial support over the (very) long process of taking this project from idea to published book. Debbie Reber also deserves my big thanks for her ongoing support and publishing know-how. I'd also like to thank Kate Rogers and Laura Shauger of Mountaineers Books, who believed in my work from the start. I'm grateful for editorial feedback and suggestions from Regan Huff, James Engelhardt, Jill McCabe Johnson, Elizabeth Johnson, Laura Kalpakian, Sandra Larkman Heindsmann, and Barbara Sjoholm.

Many friends and writers came forward with their support, critiques, and an occasional shoulder to cry on. My thanks go to Carol Raitt, Shannon Huffman Polson, Cynthia Hartwig, Sarah Corbett Morgan, Gary Presley, Judith Quaempts, Lisa Schnellinger, Daniel Becker, Steve Nicholas, Robert Goldstein, Stacy Brooks, Jagoda Perich-Anderson, Sue Muller Hacking, Brenda Peterson, Neil Mathison, Stacy Lawson, Elana Zaiman, Jennie Goode, Robyn M. Fritz, Linda Shepherd, and the late Carter Jefferson, to name a few. My apologies if I've forgotten anyone who deserves my thanks for their help.

I've been fortunate to experience excellent writing classes and workshops at Hugo House, the North Cascades Institute, and many other venues, but most importantly with Priscilla Long and the late Pesha Joyce Gertler. Priscilla's class exercises were the catalyst for what became the "Ellsworth Creek," "The Duwamish River," "East King County," and "Squire Creek" chapters. Her rigorous approach to living and working as a writer sustained me more than once during this book's creation. Pesha guided dozens (or perhaps hundreds or thousands) of Puget Sound women in their first steps toward a writing life. Pesha died shortly before *Turning Homeward* was finished, but her early instruction and inspiration are on these pages.

I spent more hours than I care to remember on Google Scholar, researching the ever-expanding field of urban nature. University of Washington Professor Thomas Quinn's *The Behavior and Ecology of Pacific Salmon and Trout* was an invaluable resource, and I am deeply grateful that he took the time to review my early drafts of the salmon chapters. I am also grateful to Professor Walter Sheppard of Washington State University who donated his time to review the chapter called "The Montlake House." Professor John Marzluff of the University of Washington generously gave his time to review the "The Montlake Fill" chapter, and his *Welcome to Subirdia* led to information and insights that deepened my book. Constance Sidles, whose book *In My Nature* was essential to my understanding the Montlake Fill, kindly gave me her time and expertise. I would also like to thank Steve Damm at the US Fish and Wildlife Service for allowing me to accompany coho pre-spawn mortality surveys along Longfellow Creek.

Thanks are also due to reviewers of earlier versions of the chapters, or those who offered information during phone or email interviews, including Don Perry of the Nisqually Indian Tribe

Salmon Recovery Program, Jennifer Vanderhoof of the King County Water and Land Resources Division, Bill Malatinsky, Julie Crittenden, and Katherine Lynch, all of Seattle Public Utilities, Robin Stanton and David Rolph of The Nature Conservancy, historian and watershed advocate Rex Ziak, Nat Scholz of NOAA's Northwest Fisheries Science Center, and Bethany Craig and Russell Link, both of the Washington Department of Fish and Wildlife, and William Dowell and Scott Pozarycki of the US Army Corps of Engineers. I'd also like to thank Peggy Foreman of NOAA's Northwest Fisheries Science Center, who assisted with a science review.

Switching from the scientific to the spiritual, several essays challenged and expanded my thinking on *tikkun olam*: Levi Cooper's "The Assimilation of Tikkun Olam," Rabbi Jill Jacobs's "Reclaiming the Reclaimed Tikkun Olam," and Hillel Halkin's "How Not to Repair the World." Rabbi Jason Levine's astute review and thoughtful comments about *tikkun olam* and Jewish practice were invaluable.

Special thanks go to Barbara Bowen and Emily Krieger for careful fact-checking, and to the Northwest Science Writers Association for introducing me to them. Any errors of fact or interpretation appearing in these pages are unintentional and solely my responsibility.

It's hard to imagine what this book would look like without Jim and Arielle's presence in my life and on these pages. They were with me along this journey, from first thoughts to eventual publication. I'm looking forward to what our next years together bring.

{ **resources** }

Stormwater and Salmon: Challenges and Opportunities

One morning I turned on my eMac before starting the day's work and opened my browser to the *Seattle PI* where I saw a headline about coho dying in restored creeks. I read what I didn't want to learn about pre-spawn mortality, and I realized what I didn't want to know, namely that restoration, if it was even possible, would be harder than I had ever imagined. I learned, too, that already underway was what would become an investigation that would continue for more than a decade by National Oceanic and Atmospheric Administration (NOAA) and other federal agencies, local government agencies, Indian tribes, salmon advocates, citizens, and citizen scientists to determine what was causing the die-offs.

By 2011, an evaluation of eight years of field research in Seattle-area streams determined that the die-offs were happening in both hatchery- and wild-origin coho, while tissue sampling showed the deaths were not caused by parasites, pathogens, or pesticides, nor by high water temperatures, low stream flows, or other indications of habitat quality. Coho did, however, show exposure to the petroleum hydrocarbons and metals associated with cars, which most likely reached the creeks via urban stormwater runoff. Subsequent geospatial analysis of six Puget Sound areas, from the relatively rural Fortson Creek to the far more industrial Longfellow Creek, showed a strong association between rates of pre-spawn mortality and the extent of nearby impervious surfaces, roads, and commercial property, establishing yet another connection between stormwater runoff and coho deaths. Models of pre-spawn mortality's impact across the region, meanwhile, suggested that the syndrome could lead to the extinction of local coho populations in anywhere from a few years to a few decades. Nor would only urban creeks be harmed. Restored creeks might act as "ecological sinks," attracting coho strays from less developed streams and eventually reducing the number of coho available to spawn in those source populations.

Finally, NOAA researchers put healthy adult coho into tanks filled with stormwater collected directly from local highways. Exposure was lethal: all the coho died, many within a few hours. Coho did survive when the stormwater in their tanks was first filtered by flowing it through columns containing layers of gravel, sand, compost, and mulched bark, the basic components of a rain garden.

Soil infiltration like this is used in green stormwater infrastructure (low-impact development, or LID), which recreates the way forests, wetlands, and other natural systems capture rainfall and slowly allow it to soak into the ground. Common techniques include rain gardens, rain cisterns, permeable paving, and many other inexpensive ways of having our homes and neighborhoods eliminate or reduce stormwater's impact. Across Washington State, new stormwater regulations require that cities and counties above a certain size move toward green stormwater infrastructure in managing runoff. As NOAA's research showed, even a simple rain garden in a backyard can make an enormous contribution toward protecting salmon, and from there our creeks and waterways, and Puget Sound.

To learn more about NOAA's research, visit the **Northwest Fisheries Science Center's** "Stormwater Science: Ecological Impacts" page at www.nwfsc.noaa.gov/research/divisions/efs/ecotox/ecoimpacts.cfm. If you want to understand the science behind NOAA's stormwater-focused studies, check out these publications:

Feist, Blake, et al., "Landscape Ecotoxicology of Coho Salmon Spawner Mortality in Urban Streams." *PLoS ONE* 6, no. 8 (2011): e23424.

Scholz, Nathaniel, et al., "Recurrent Die-Offs of Adult Coho Salmon Returning to Spawn in Puget Sound Lowland Urban Streams." *PLoS ONE* 6, no. 12 (2011): e28013.

Spromberg, Julann, and Nathaniel Scholz, "Estimating the Future Decline of Wild Coho Salmon Populations Resulting from Early Spawner Die-Offs in Urbanizing Watersheds of the Pacific Northwest, USA." *Integrated Environmental Assessment and Management* 7, no. 4 (2011): 648–656.

Spromberg, Julann, et al., "Coho Salmon Spawner Mortality in Western US Urban Watersheds: Bioinfiltration Prevents Lethal Stormwater Impacts." *Journal of Applied Ecology* 53 (2016): 398–407.

Rain Gardens and Green Stormwater Infrastructure

Washington State University Extension offers an excellent overview of rain gardens: http://ext100.wsu.edu/raingarden. In conjunction with the WA Department of Ecology, they published *Rain Garden Handbook for Western Washington—A Guide for Design, Installation, and Maintenance*, a free publication available at www.700milliongallons.org/wp-content/uploads/2015/04/Rain-Garden-Handbook-for-Western-Washington.pdf that covers basic design and installation. One of the authors of WSU's handbook, Zsofia Pasztor, has also coauthored a more detailed guide, *Rain Gardens in the Pacific Northwest: Design and Build Your Own*, forthcoming from Skipstone in January 2017. The **Sightline Institute**, www.sightline.org/series/stormwater-solutions-curbing-toxic-runoff, is a good resource for learning about stormwater issues, as well as LID methods such as rain gardens. In a report focused on policy and implementation titled *Low-Impact Development/Green Stormwater Infrastructure Lay of the Land Report: On-the-Ground Realities in King County*, **Futurewise**, www.futurewise.wa.org, presents the challenges and possibilities of implementing green stormwater infrastructure on a local level.

A free downloadable guide put together for Seattle residents by the **Seattle Public Utilities** and the **King County Wastewater Treatment Division**, "Right Place, Right Project—A Community Guide to Partnership Opportunities," www.700milliongallons.org/wp-content/uploads/2015/08/RightPlaceRightProject.pdf, explores the many green stormwater infrastructure techniques that will work best for your home or neighborhood, from rain gardens to green roofs, permeable paving and depaving, as well as possible funding sources for neighborhood-level projects. The **Washington Stormwater Center**, www.wastormwatercenter.org/home, a collaboration between Washington State University–Puyallup and the Center for Urban Waters at the University of Washington–Tacoma, is a statewide resource on stormwater and LID offering an online library, trainings and workshops, research on emerging low-impact methods, information on watershed planning, and much more, largely focused on helping municipalities and businesses better understand and manage stormwater runoff.

To start using rain gardens and other green stormwater infrastructure in your home or neighborhood, visit **12,000 Rain Gardens in Puget Sound**, www.12000raingardens.org. This joint campaign of **Stewardship Partners,** www.stewardshippartners.org, and the Washington State University Extension, http://extension .wsu.edu, has a goal of creating 12,000 rain gardens in neighborhoods across Puget Sound, enough to soak up an estimated 160 million gallons of polluted stormwater each year. This site will give you a solid start for installing a rain garden in your home or community, whether by building one yourself or by hiring from their list of qualified professionals. Their website also lists restoration events, workshops for professionals or volunteers, key governmental or local nonprofit partners, and special information for schools or community groups.

Depave, http://depave.org, helps local people remove unneeded concrete and other impervious surfaces from their community and replace it with community gardens and other public spaces. While most of their resources are specific to Portland, Oregon, where they are based, their free, downloadable guide "How to Depave: The Guide to Freeing Your Soil," is available at http://depave.org /learn/how-to-depave, and also applies to the Puget Sound region.

To find contractors in the Seattle area trained in rain garden and other green stormwater installation and learn more about rebates, grants, or other financial incentives for using green stormwater techniques, check out **RainWise**, www.700million gallons.org/rainwise, which awards qualifying Seattle residents a substantial rebate for installing a rain garden or cistern. If you live in the larger Puget Sound region or elsewhere in the state, learn more about incentive programs at **12,000 Rain Gardens**, www.12000raingardens.org/about-rain -gardens-incentives. If you are in either Bellingham and Whatcom County, consult the "2012 Whatcom County Low-Impact Development Resource Guide," www.12000raingardens.org/wp-content /uploads/2013/05/2012-LowImpact-Resource-Guide_SC.pdf.

Citizen Science and Restoration-Focused Opportunities

To find hands-on restoration activities, check out this small sampling of the local, regional, statewide, or national organizations dedicated to citizen science and restoration: **EarthCorps**, www.earthcorps.org/volunteer-program.php, volunteer projects include nearshore restoration, citizen science and forest monitoring, invasive species removal, restoration-focused international exchanges, and many other projects in the Puget Sound region. **The Dirt**, www.kingcounty.gov/services/environment /stewardship/volunteer.aspx, is an online calendar of hands-on restoration projects in King County. Other opportunities can be found at **Volunteer for Salmon**, www.govlink.org/watersheds/8 /action/Volunteer.aspx. **Forterra**, http://forterra.org, runs many restoration and policy-focused projects including Green City Partnerships, http://forterra.org/service/green-city-partnerships, which offers hands-on, local restoration opportunities in Everett, Kent, Kirkland, Puyallup, Redmond, Seattle (a.k.a. Green Seattle Partnership), and Tacoma (a.k.a. Green Tacoma Partnership), and potentially more Puget Sound cities.

Adopt A Stream Foundation, www.streamkeeper.org/aasf /Welcome.html, offers restoration opportunities in the Snohomish and Sammamish river tributaries, as well as coastal stream stewardship programs, environmental education, and many other restoration-focused activities. **Regional Fisheries Enhancement Groups** (RFEGs), http://wdfw.wa.gov/about/volunteer/rfeg/, are nonprofit organizations initially created by the Washington State Legislature to involve local communities, landowners, tribes, and other grassroots stakeholders in local, watershed-based salmon restoration efforts. Some volunteer opportunities include salmon or water quality monitoring, tree planting, habitat assessments, and other tasks best suited to a particular watershed. The Washington Department of Fish and Wildlife's Volunteer Opportunities/ RFEGs webpage has contact information for 14 RFEGs across Washington, including many in the Puget Sound region.

Audubon Washington, http://wa.audubon.org/ways-help /birds-and-citizen-science, offers bird-focused citizen science conservation work across the state, some in conjunction with the Cornell Lab of Ornithology, a leader in citizen science projects. The **Citizen Science Association** (CSA), http://citizenscience .org, is a growing network of organizations and individuals engaging local people in citizen science. While it is not a place to learn about specific volunteer opportunities, CSA does offer conferences, a journal, and other ways of sharing ideas and information. **SciStarter**, http://scistarter.com, is another place to find and participate in citizen science activities. Their growing searchable database lists projects happening on the local, regional, national, and even international level.

JAMES SCANLAN

Adrienne Ross Scanlan has explored the Pacific Northwest (inside and outside the city) as a lay naturalist, restoration volunteer, and citizen scientist. From these and other experiences have come essays published in *City Creatures Blog*, the *Fourth River*, *Pilgrimage*, *Under the Sun*, anthologies such as the *American Nature Writing* series and *A Natural History of Now: Reports from the Edge of Nature*, and other publications.

She's an Artist Trust Fellowship recipient, backyard city farmer, and not-too-bad chess player who loves to hike and dance. She lives in Seattle with her husband and daughter. Learn more about Adrienne at http://adrienne-ross-scanlan.com.

MOUNTAINEERS BOOKS including its two imprints, Skipstone and Braided River, is a leading publisher of quality outdoor recreation, sustainability, and conservation titles. As a 501(c)(3) nonprofit, we are committed to supporting the environmental and educational goals of our organization by providing expert information on human-powered adventure, sustainable practices at home and on the trail, and preservation of wilderness.

Our publications are made possible through the generosity of donors, and through sales of more than 600 titles on outdoor recreation, sustainable lifestyle, and conservation. To donate, purchase books, or learn more, visit us online:

MOUNTAINEERS BOOKS
1001 SW Klickitat Way, Suite 201 • Seattle, WA 98134
800-553-4453 • mbooks@mountaineersbooks.org • www.mountaineersbooks.org

OTHER MOUNTAINEERS BOOKS TITLES YOU MAY ENJOY!